C000197577

ROCHFORD
A History

North Street, looking south. The tall house on the left is the old Fire House.

ROCHFORD
A History

Mavis Sipple

Phillimore

2004

Published by
PHILLIMORE & CO. LTD
Shopwyke Manor Barn, Chichester, West Sussex, England

ISBN 1 86077 310 9

Printed and bound in Great Britain by
CROMWELL PRESS

Contents

To
Pete and Sarah

List of Illustrations

Frontispiece: North Street, looking south.

Acknowledgements

The illustrations in this book are reproduced by courtesy of the following: Mary Avis, 131; Margaret Benham, 84, 106; Anne Boulter, 140; Michael Bull, 24; Margaret Chambers, 36; Ken Crowe, 1; Sheila Dowell, 32, 38, 51, 70, 87, 120, 127-30, 138; Essex Police Museum, 65, 69; Essex Record Office, 12, 25, 31, 46, 54, 60-1, 64, 67, 71-2, 75, 78, 90, 92, 100; Ruth Harley, 53; Barbara Burbridge Jones, 79-80; Sheridan Newman, 52; Betty Noakes, 123, 126; Staff at the Old House, 8, 10; Jan Pallett, 116; Helen Porter, 101-2; Staff of Rochford Primary School, 85; Rochford W.I., 146; Valerie Smerdon, 108; Neil Smith, 44-5; Arthur Stephenson, 104-5; Mrs Whittingham, 114-15, 125; Sue Williams, from the *Golden Lion*, 50.

I would like to thank the following for their help and encouragement: Ann Cross, Doreen Armstrong, Gwyneth and Doreen Sparrow, Janet over the road, Jeremy Squier, John Lewzey, Maurice Drage, Mrs Squier, Neil Vinall, Pete Sipple, Roy Andrews, Sarah Shawcross, Sharon Taplin, Sylvia Drage, Mr Wall, Derek Childs and Staff at the Masonic Hall, Staff of Rochford Golf Club, Rochford Library Staff (especially Susan Gough and Toby Evans), and Southend Library Staff, Brian Shannon, Cy Rampersaud and the staff at Rochford County Primary School.

And more particularly Brenda Poole, for the work she put in, Jill Henderson, Meriel Kennedy, Maureen McCourt and Melody Hurst, from the Southend Record Office, for their help and advice, and Sheila Dowell for generously lending me the many photos and pictures from her collection. Also Jan Pallett, Mrs Whittingham, Maureen Benham, Betty Noakes, Sherry Newman and Helen Porter, for kindly allowing me to use some of their photos, and Eric Gooch for permitting me to use his paintings.

One

The Early Days

The Romans

The earliest evidence of settlement in Rochford was found when building work was in progress at the hospital. A number of Roman bricks and mosaic tiles were unearthed, so it is very probable that there had been a quite large Roman building in the area. However, it is almost certain that there was a community in Rochford much earlier than Roman times. Hand axes dating back to the Palaeolithic, or early Stone Age, have been discovered at nearby Stambridge. Celtic coins have been found in the River Roach. Flint tools from the Neolithic (late Stone Age) have been found in Stambridge and Canewdon. Pieces of Grooveware pottery from the late Neolithic period have been discovered at Stambridge.

Rochford and the surrounding area, with its desolate marshland and hundreds of tiny inlets, was an ideal place to settle, the land was fertile, and the river close at hand for transport, salt making and for fishing. The local oysters were plentiful and considered to be the best in the country. The flat marshlands were ideal for grazing sheep, which supplied wool, skins, mutton and dairy produce, especially huge cheeses made from ewe's milk, which were a speciality of the area. It is likely that from very early days Rochford was a thriving port with boats taking produce to London.

Marshall's Farm on the Southend Road was built on the site of a Roman farm. Finds at Purdey's Estate, just south of the town, include Roman pots and what is thought to be a branding iron. Roman pottery has been found in East Street.

1 Flagon, beaker and iron lamp holder from Roman times found at Purdey's Estate.

The Saxons

There were Saxon settlements in the area but so far no Saxon artefacts have been found in Rochford. The various Anglo-Saxon kingdoms were divided into hundreds of which there were 14 in Essex. The Rochford Hundred was mainly woodland, and it covered about 60,000 acres of land between the River Crouch and the Thames, and from the North Sea as far west as Raweth. It was made up of a number of parishes. The hundreds were formed in 973 by King Edgar the Peaceful (or Peaceable). Their main purpose was to control each manor for the good of its inhabitants. The fact that

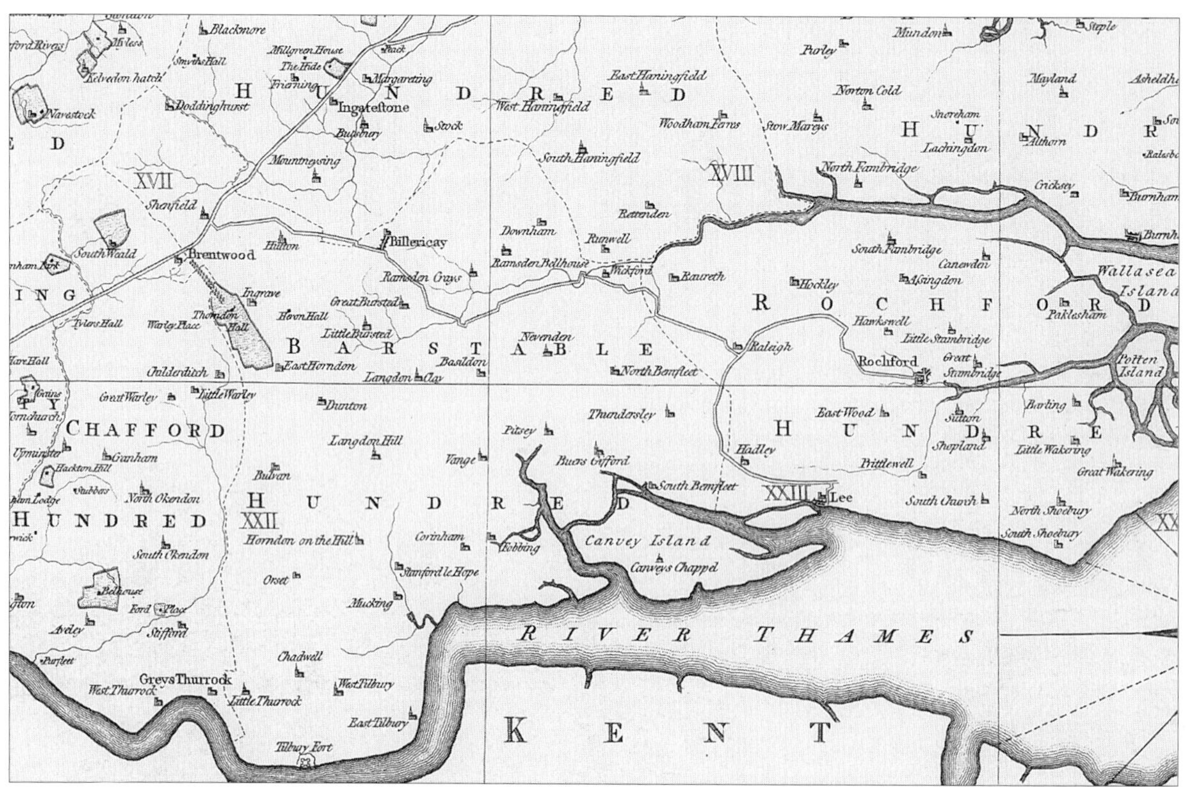

2 Key map to Rochford Hundred and south-west Essex, surveyed by Chapman and André, 1777.

Rochford was chosen as the name for the hundred shows that it was already an important place. Just a short distance away, Canewdon takes its name from the Saxon. The oldest part of the parish church contains many Roman bricks, probably from the previous church.

St Peter's Church, Paglesham, built by the Normans, also stands on the site of an earlier Saxon church. Ashingdon Church claims to have been built on the site of a Saxon establishment dating from around 970. The present church is reputed to have been built by King Cnut. The son of Sweyn, the Danish king was determined to conquer England. After many attempts he confronted the English army, led by Edmund of Assendun, on Assendun Hill. It is thought that one of the English commanders defected to the enemy, causing the rest to panic. They were defeated and Cnut became king. After his victory at Assendun he is said to have built the minster of stone and lime for the souls of the men slain in the fierce battle. Inside the church is a model of a Viking ship given to the church by the people of Denmark, who helped restore the nave roof. Georg, Prince of Denmark attended the consecration service in 1951 and presented the church with a Danish flag, which is now hanging in the chancel. There is some controversy over the location of the Battle of Assendun, another contender for that honour being Ashden.

The Normans

There are several theories concerning the name 'Rochford'. Some say it means 'the ford of the hunting dog', others that it is the 'ford over the rocks'. Another theory is that it was named after the fish (roach) that abound in the river,

3 St Andrew's Church, Ashingdon Minster, was built by King Cnut for the souls of the men slain in the battle of Assendun.

Rochefort ten& Alured de . S . qd ten . I . lib hō . t . r . e . p . m̄ . 7 p . II . hid . 7 . dim . Sēp . v . uilt . Tc̄ . IIII . bor . m̊ . XII . Tc̄ . II . ser . m̊ . III tc̄ . II . car in dn̄io . m̊ . III . Tc̄ . III . car . hom . m̊ . IIII . 7 . I . lib hō ten& . XXX . ac . 7 adhuc jacent huic man . II . ac̄ pti . Silu . XX . porc . I . mol . Tc̄ . I . runc . 7 . VIII . porc . 7 . XI . ou . m̊ . III . runc . 7 . II . pult . 7 . X . an . 7 . XXI . porc . 7 . CLX . ou . 7 XXIII . ou . Tc̄ ualuit . c . sol . m̊ . VII . lib.	Alfred holds ROCHFORD from Swein which 1 free man held before 1066 as a manor, for 2½ hides. Always 5 villagers. Then 4 smallholders, now 12; then 2 slaves, now 3. Then 2 ploughs, in lordship, now 3. Then 3 men's ploughs, now 4. 1 Free man holds 30 acres and they also lie in (hands of) this manor. Meadow, 2 acres; woodland, 20 pigs; 1 mill. Then 1 cob, 8 pigs and 11 sheep; now 3 cobs, 2 foals, 10 cattle, 21 pigs, 160 sheep and 23 sheep. Value then 100s; now £7.
Stanbruge ten& Wiard de . S . qd tenuit . I . lib hō . t . r . e . p . uno man . 7 . p . I . hid . 7 . dim 7 . VII . ac . 7 . dim . Sēp . II . bord . 7 . I . ser . 7 . dim . car . tc̄ : m̊ . I . Past . c . ou . Tc̄ ual . X . sol . m̊ . XXV.	Wicard holds (Great) STAMBRIDGE from Swein, which 1 free man held before 1066 as one manor, for 1½ hides and 7½ acres. Always 2 smallholders; 1 slave. ½ plough then, now 1. Pasture, 100 sheep. Value then 10s; now 25[s].

4 Rochford and Stambridge are both mentioned in Domesday Book.

5 The model Viking ship, donated by the Danish people who had helped to restore the nave, hangs in Ashingdon church.

6 The 14th-century Rochford church, dedicated to St Andrew, patron saint of fishermen and mariners.

and the ford that crossed it. However the name came about, it is certain that Rochford was an important town. Victorious King William carried out a survey to find out exact details of every parish in the country and the resulting Domesday Book records that the manor of 'Rochefort' was held by one freeman at the time of King Edward, but by 1086 by Alured of Suene. The community consisted of about twenty households but it is unclear where it was located. It is thought the early settlement probably clustered around the area where the church now stands. The present church was built in about the 14th century most probably on the site of an earlier one. The moated manor house stood near the church. The present town grew up half a mile from the church and manor.

The next written reference to Rochford is in 1264, when the lord of the manor, Sir Guy de Rochford, obtained a grant of a market and fair from King Henry III. The exact location is not known, but during restoration work carried out on the present Market Square in the 1980s, postholes were uncovered, cut into the gravel, which were from light timber buildings. Above the gravel were clay surfaces from low clay walls, suggesting small shops or workshops.

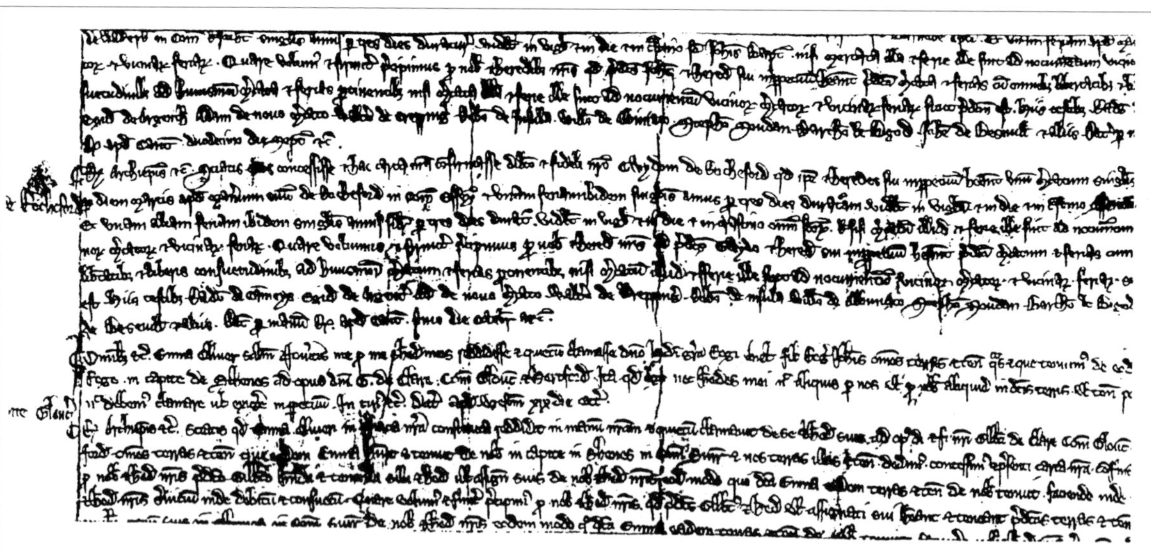

7 The market charter was granted by lord of the manor Sir Guy de Rochford in 1264.

8 The Old House in South Street dates back to about 1270.

These had been renewed several times over the years. In the layers of gravel, pottery from about the 13th century was found. Pottery also from the 13th century was discovered in what is thought to be a roadside ditch near the present market site. It is, therefore, thought that the present market is held on the same site as the original one. It is certain that the Market Square was a thriving place in the 13th century; it was much bigger then, incorporating the wedge-shaped Horner's Corner. Several layers of gravel containing coal, cockle and oyster shells were discovered, and part of a clay oven and pieces of querns (lava stones used for grinding corn) were found in one corner. The River Crouch was famous for its oyster grounds and the marshlands were ideal for sheep rearing, supplying wool, skins, cheeses and mutton for the London market during the Saxon period.

A short way from the market, halfway down South Street, is number 17, the Old House, Rochford's oldest building, sometimes called the Pink House or the Moot House. This fine

9 The great chimney was added to the Old House in the 16th century.

10 This drawing shows what the house may have looked like by about 1400.

dwelling built in *c.*1270 is thought to have been one of a row of houses in what was the main road to the Priory at Prittlewell. The timber-framed house, built on stone foundations, had one big room with a clay floor covered with rushes. In the middle of the room was an open hearth made of tiles with a wooden kerb to keep the logs in place and a small flue in the roof to allow the smoke to escape. This was where the family and their servants lived. Their only source of light and heat was the great fire. The master and his family would have taken their meals at a table on a raised platform at one end of the room, the servants using tables along the sides of the walls which would have doubled as beds. There was probably a separate room at one end for use as a bedchamber by the master. Twenty years later an extension was added on the north end. The wooden frame was infilled with wattle and daub, a network of sticks and twigs bound together with clay, mud and straw. An extension on the south side was built about a hundred years later. From the quality of the building work and the materials used, it is obvious that this was once the home of a very prosperous man. The magnificent chimney was installed in the early 16th century. One of the extensions or crosswings may have been used as a shop in early times.

It was certainly a shop during the 18th century when it was owned by George Garrett, Chandler of Rochford. Around this time a large bay window was added. After his death his wife carried on the business for another twenty years. In 1826 the trades directory lists George Turner, boot and shoemaker, in residence. From 1855 to 1902 John Hedgecock ran the boot and shoemaker's business, which was also a stationer's and fancy goods shop.

Two

The Hall

The church was the most important building in any town or village, the size of the building reflecting the prosperity of the area. Rochford's ancient parish church, named after St Andrew, patron saint of fishermen and mariners, dates back to the late 13th or early 14th century but there was a much earlier church on the site. The list of incumbents shows that Simon Mansell was vicar in 1219. The parish priest was maintained by tithes, part of the corn, hay, fruit, eggs, wood and stock produced by the parish. By the mid-19th century, these tithes had become monetary payments.

The next building of importance was the Manor House. Originally the manor referred to all the land held by the lord from the king in return for services, and worked by peasants who were given a small piece of

11 St Andrew's Church, Rochford was built on the site of an older church.

C.C.—London: Printed and Published (By Authority,) by Shaw and Sons, 137 & 138, Fetter-lane.

LANDOWNERS.	OCCUPIERS.	Numbers referring to the Plan.	NAME AND DESCRIPTION OF LANDS AND PREMISES.	STATE OF CULTIVATION.	QUANTITIES IN STATUTE MEASURE. A.	R.	P.	Amount of Rent-Charge apportioned upon the several Lands, and Payable to Rector. £.	s.	d.	REMARKS.
Harridge David	James Keyes	225		Arable	3	.	34	1	8	.	
Baker William and Dollen Abel Ross	Thomas Merryfield	264	Barn Mead	pasture	7	3	11				
		265	Kitchen Mead	ditto	5	.	28				
		266	Eight Acres	ditto	7	2	.				
		267	Cottage and Garden		.	1	36				
		268	Offices &c Great Brays		1	.	13				
		269	Cottage and Garden		.	.	16				
					22	.	24	6	.	.	
Dowter John	John Dowter	271	Little Brays Offices Yards &c		.	1	31				
		272	Cottage and Garden		.	1	25				
		273		pasture	4	1	30				
		274		Arable	11	.	32				
		275		ditto	7	.	22				
					23	2	20	1	9	5	
	Wm White Gillingham	308	House Yard &c		.	.	21				
Cockerton William	Thomas Coolbear	276	Golden Cross House & Garden		.	.	21				
		277		Garden & Orchard	.	1	29				
		278	Offices Pond &c		1	.	30				
		279		Arable	4	2	31				
		280		pasture	3	.	26				
		281		Arable	8	.	3				
		282		ditto	9	1	30				
					27	.	10		10	19	
Copsey William	Thomas Smith	300	Crown Inn Yard &c		.	.	10				
	John Le Grys	301	Cottage		.	.	1½				
	William Copsey	302	Cottage and Yard		.	.	3½				
					.	.	15				
Townsend Charles	William Salmon	304	Cottage Offices and Yards		.	.	24½				
Townsend Barnabas	Barnabas Townsend	305	Potash Kiln		.	.	18½				
Thorn John	John Thorn	307	House and Garden		1	.	21				
		342		pasture	.	.	17				
					1	.	38		.	10	

12 Each landowner was obliged to make payments for the upkeep of the parish. Tithes due in the year 1837 show that wheat was valued at 7s. a bushel, barley at 3s. 11½d., oats at 2s. 9d.

land for their own use. They paid taxes to the lord. The Manor of Rochford came into the possession of James Boteler, 4th Earl of Ormonde in about 1460. James had the old stone manor house pulled down and began to build the magnificent Rochford Hall. Part of the work was destroyed when a fire broke out in the chapel after candles set fire to the altar hangings. So it was quite a modest building when James, ardent supporter of the Lancastrians, was captured after a battle against the Yorkists and was beheaded. The manor returned to the Crown.

Rochford was eventually restored to the Boteler family and in 1485 Sir Thomas Boteler was the owner of the Hall. He added to the building and also built the impressive tower of the parish church using local bricks. Thomas amassed a huge fortune and in his will he left half his 72 mansions to each of his two daughters. Rochford went to Margaret, who was married into the Boleyn family. Her son Thomas Boleyn became owner of the Hall in 1515. Boleyn was extremely wealthy and it is probable that he carried on with the building of the great hall. While the Boleyn family lived here, their daughter Anne became the second wife of King Henry VIII and mother of Elizabeth, later Queen Elizabeth I. Their other daughter Mary was married to Sir William Stafford, who was renowned for taking the bells from local churches to repair the sea

13 The Hall replaced the original stone manor house in the 16th century.

walls. Three bells were taken from the church at Rochford, and one from Hawkwell. There is no record of the money being used to make the sea walls safer.

The Hall was willed to Mary when her father died. It was she who requested that there should be a dovecote in the grounds. The dove house, one of the first to be built in the county, was circular, about forty feet in diameter with a conical thatched roof. It was built in the little meadow to the south of the great house in 1540. There was a door at one side and a trap in the roof worked by pulleys so the birds could be let out or kept in as required. The house held about three hundred birds, a valuable source of meat during the winter months. Every bit of the bird was used: the eggs were eaten, the feathers used in pillows, and the dung for fertiliser and a cure for gout and fever, as well as being a restorative. In later years the dovecote became very dilapidated and was used for storage and as a pigsty. In 1888 it was struck by lightning and had to be pulled down. The grounds of the Hall were vast: at the north-east corner, according to Benton, was an ancient brick and tile summerhouse; the wilderness behind the church was a beautiful retreat with shrubs and bushes.

The next owner of the Hall was Mary's son Henry; he sold the property to Lord Rich in 1552. The Rich family carried on with the

14 The Causeway, now named West Street. On the right are the Almshouses built by the Rich family for six poor people of the parish.

building of the magnificent mansion, using stone thought to have come from churches and monasteries destroyed after the Dissolution. The Hall was one of the largest in the country, and some of its outer walls were three feet thick. Some of them were without foundations. It was surrounded by acres of parkland and a defensive wall, complete with slits for arrows and blunderbusses, was built around the property. The Rich family also built on to the church tower.

In his will of 1567 Robert Rich left £60 for the building of almshouses for some of the poor people of Rochford. These were built by his grandson nearly fifty years later, six one-roomed houses with a large garden quite close to the Hall. They were given for the use of six poor people for ever, five of whom should be aged, poor, lame or impotent, and the sixth an ancient woman, fit and able to look after the others. Rich willed that two good loads of timber cut from his own woods should be delivered to them every year. The upkeep of the properties would be carried out by the Hall, the inmates cared for by the parish. The Rich family owned the Hall from 1552 until 1673 and during this time they acquired a great deal of land throughout Essex.

15 The *King's Head* takes its name from Henry VIII, who spent time at the Hall and hunting in the Forest when he was courting Anne Boleyn. It was here that the feast took place on the night of the Whispering Court.

After the Rich family Rochford's great Hall had many owners, each one adding to its structure, until around 1760, when it was at its most magnificent, and a great fire started in the attics and swept rapidly through the rooms, so badly destroying the south wing that most of it had to be pulled down. The west wing was badly damaged and became fit only to be used as barns. Part of the Hall remained habitable, but it was now reduced in size and had only 18 bedrooms. The great Hall with its turrets, gables and twisting chimneys, which had taken over two hundred years to build, lay mainly in ruins for another two centuries.

It was while the 2nd Earl of Warwick was living at Rochford Hall that the venue for the famous Whispering Court was changed. It had originally been held at Kings in Rayleigh but the earl decided it should be transferred to Kings Hill, Rochford because 'he would have it so'. The court started when the lord of the manor, returning home late one night and hearing some of his tenants whispering, listened and found they were plotting against him. He also heard a cock crowing. Furious with the tenants, he decreed that every year they should meet and pay homage to him. Originally there were two courts, the Little Lawless Court, which was held on Rope Monday, the second Monday after Easter, and the Great Lawless Court held on the Wednesday after the feast of Saint Michael, at the end of September. In time only one court was held. On the appointed day, according to Benton, the Essex historian, a great feast was held at the *King's Head*. As it was nearing midnight, the chairman put on his coat and went to the door to listen. A man appeared outside carrying over his shoulder

16 The blue plaque on Rochford Hall presented by Rochford Hundred Historical Society.

17 The Lawless, or Whispering Court took place outside this building, King's Hill.

18 The whispering post is found at King's Hill and must be preserved forever.

a brand, blazing for a foot and a half of its length, then came others carrying links; the chairman and his guests would follow them up the road amidst the local lads cock crowing for all their might. When they arrived at the place of penance, a grassy meadow, the tenants would kneel down around a white post carved from wood, the top resembling the flame of a candle. The steward said in a whisper the names of the tenants, who had to reply 'Here Sir' or be fined for every hour they were absent. Then the steward declared, 'Oh yes, Oh yes, all persons have leave to depart. God Save the Queen.' The firebrand was put out at the foot of the post, a burnt piece of wood was taken from the fire to make a tally on the post, and the link bearers rushed forward and beat their torches against the post to extinguish them. Amidst the 'great clamour of cock a hoops', the members of the court returned to the inn for another bowl of punch.

Most of the farms in the area were in the homage of the court of Rochford Hall. The homage was a pledge of loyalty, sworn by the tenant to the lord of the manor. Acceptance of a tenant obliged the lord to warrant him. The tenant placed his hands between those of the lord and said, 'I become your man from this day forth for life.'

Three

The Farms

Rochford Hall Farm was the biggest and most important of the farms in the area, occupying as much land as all the other farms on the Rochford Estate. The land was fertile and suitable for cereal crops, potatoes and mustard. The farmers trod their land with horses and bullocks to guard against wire worm, and took the hunt over their land to help fertilise it. Most of them were very superstitious and would never sow oats on Ash Wednesday and always sowed cole at night to avoid the fly. Mr Barrington of Doggetts, and others, used to set fire to the weeds at the risk of burning down their farmhouses. The flat marshy land was used for sheep rearing.

The manor of Great Doggetts was held in 1305 by Robert Doggett and Alice, his wife. The farm, which was situated partly in Rochford and partly in Stambridge, was next in importance to Rochford Hall Farm. Great Doggetts consisted of over eighty acres of arable land stretching from Weir Pond Road to Brays Lane, and from Ashingdon Road to Stambridge. The farmhouse was very fine with large gardens, an ornamental lake and five cottages. Near one of the cottages was the bobbing pond where the witches and wayward women were ducked. Generally speaking, Lincoln sheep were reared in the area but, according to Mrs Jerram-Burrows (*Bygone Rochford*, Phillimore, 1988), sheep from Romney Marsh in Kent were introduced at Doggetts, which is how part of the farm became known as Romney Marsh. One notable occupier of Great Doggetts was Stephen Jackson, High Constable of the Rochford Hundred. Doggetts was sold to Mr W.H. Meeson for £18,000 at the sale of the Rochford Hall estate and in 1917 the Squier family bought the farm from Mr Meeson, including Romney Marsh. When the sand and gravel had been extracted from the Romney

19 Map of 1897 showing Doggetts Farm, Great Brays, and Coombs Farm which was on Stambridge Road.

Marsh meadow, the 13 acres of land was made over to Rochford Rural District Council.

Part of the farm in the parish of Canewdon, was known as Little Doggetts. The 121 acres had been in the same hands for many years and the rent was £130. It was sold to Henry Mew for £7,500 when the Rochford Estate was sold in 1867.

Swaines Farm was partly divided by Ashingdon Road. The smaller part north of Ironwell Lane included the house and 33 acres and was situated in Hawkwell. Swaines (or Swaynes) was part of the estate of Lord Rich

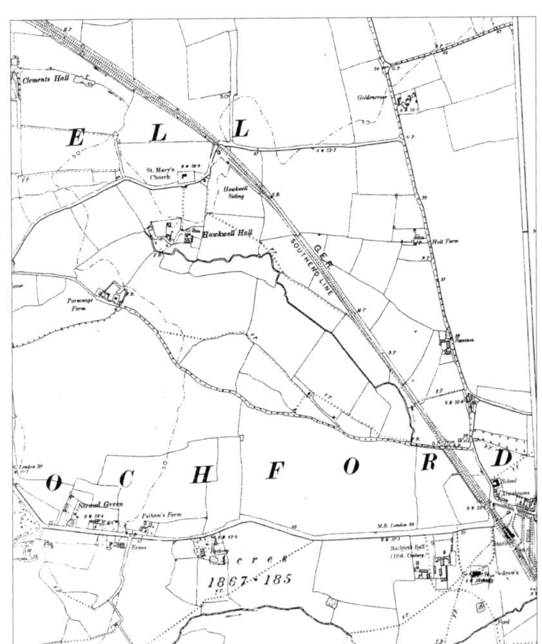

20 This map shows Rochford Hall, Swaines and Pelham's Farms, as well as the Rectory on Hall Road.

21 The Avenue ran adjacent to Rochford Hall Farm.

22 Weir Pond Road, looking towards North Street.

at the Hall. The house, garden, brewhouse, meadowlands and farm buildings were let to James Cockerton, who bought them when the estate was sold in 1867. The other part of Swaines ran from Ashingdon Road to Doggetts. This was also rented by James Cockerton. According to Benton, the Earl of Mornington bequeathed it to Lord Cowley who sold 83 acres to William Taylor Meeson. The remaining 33 acres and farmhouse were sold to Mr Meeson some time later.

Coombes or Blue House Farm stretched from the Roach to Stambridge and was 136 acres. The house in Little Stambridge was once a manor house surrounded by a moat. At one time it was leased to Thomas Bullen's daughter, Mary Carey. Later it went to the Earl of Mornington, who sold it in 1867 for £6,860 to John Offord, proprietor of the *King's Head*, who sold part to Arthur Carey. The steam works were built there. Another part was made into a brickfield. Mill Lane led through the property from Rochford to the mill at Stambridge.

Great Brays Farm stretched from Brays Lane into Ashingdon, Hawkwell and Little Stambridge. The farm changed hands several times before it was bought by William Taylor Meeson of Great Doggetts. In 1828 it was leased to Merryfield of Rochford, a maltster. The wooden house with its thatched roof, large pond and various outbuildings was later bought by Mr Bull. The Bull family ran Great Brays Fruit Farm from 1942 until 1997.

23 Barges took their loads from Stambridge Mill to London.

24 Mr Bull outside Great Brays Fruit Farm.

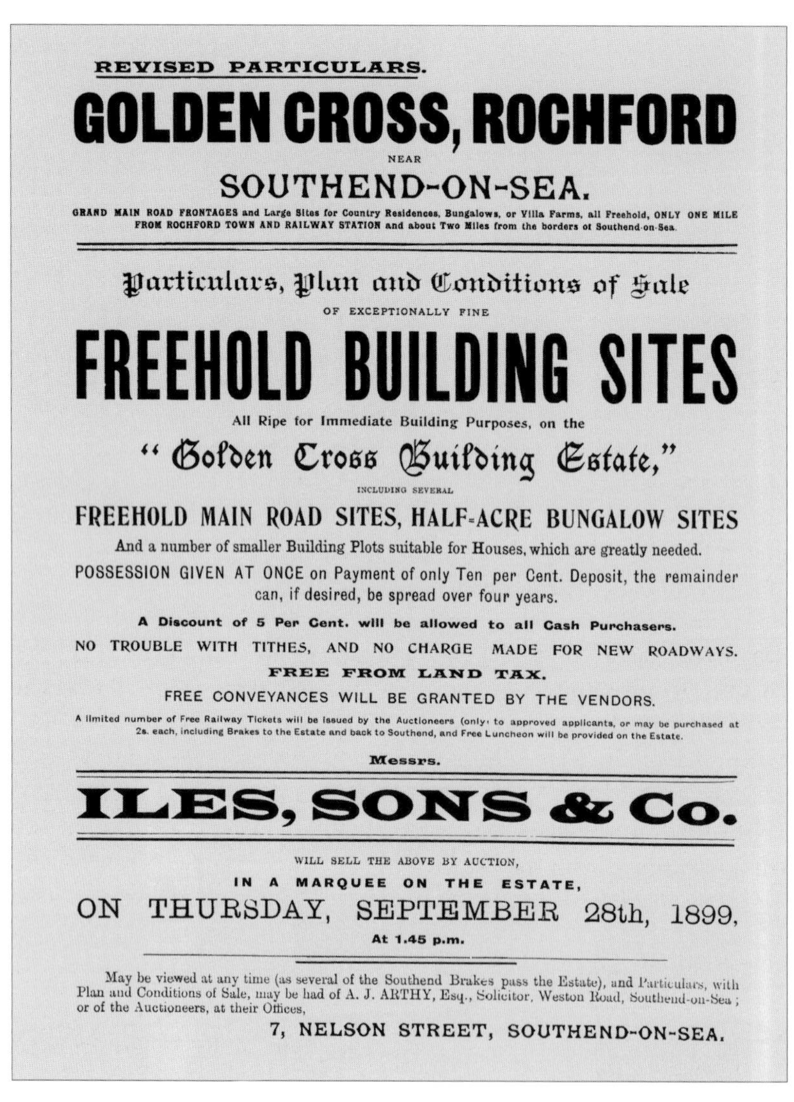

25 Golden Cross housing estate was built on land formerly belonging to Golden Cross Farm.

Stroud Green House, later named the Lawn, is at the far end of the parish. The farm house was once the *Mother Shipton* and the coach road was originally in front of the property. When Mr Carr lived there he enclosed part of the common, diverted the road, and built a fine house in front of the old inn. When Arthur Tawke owned the property he pulled down the old building and extended the house. At that time the property consisted of 175 acres and Potash Wood. The *Cock* inn took over from the *Mother Shipton*. Golden Cross Farm off Ashingdon Road was owned by Gilbert de Goldlay in the 13th century and by W.J. Cockerton. Mr Rankin later bought the farm, a cottage, outbuildings, a well and pump and land covering over 63 acres. It was sold in 1898 for £900, and the Golden Cross housing estate now occupies the land.

Four

The Parish

The parish was governed by the vestry, parish officers being responsible for its efficient administration. Two were elected and it was their duty to collect and administer communal funds. Two annually elected churchwardens were the representatives of the parishioners and were responsible for church property. Meetings held in the church were open to all ratepayers. In 1642 parish registers were instituted which were to give a precise record of all baptisms, marriages and burials. Records were kept by the parish clerk, often in a rather haphazard way, on odd sheets of paper which were mislaid often, misspelt or written incorrectly. The overseer of Prittlewell parish wrote a short history of the parish register at the back of his register: 'In 1597, the 39th year of Elizabeth, all entries that were extant were to be copied into vellum books provided at the expense of the parish. Each page attested by the vicar and churchwarden, to be started in 1558.' By 1604 it was ordered that duplicates should be made and sent to Bishop's Registry of the diocese, but nearly all the Essex duplicates were destroyed in the Great Fire of London in 1666.

Some clerks added interesting details to the entries. Prittlewell's register includes Mary Bush of Temple Farm, who hanged herself and was buried at the backside of the church where criminals, suicides and the unbaptised were buried and considered to be the Devil's side. The register also mentions Mary Smith, buried in the churchyard at Rochford in wool, an affidavit being brought. Prompted by the declining wool trade, Charles II passed the Flannel Act, which stated that people must be buried in a woollen shroud and not, as was usual and cheaper, in linen. Unfortunately, Rochford's records note just the name, age and date.

Another responsibility of the parish was caring for the aged, infirm and poor. The 16th-century Poor Laws gave the parish overseer the task of allocating relief to the sick, needy, and destitute children and providing work for the able-bodied in the workhouse. Paupers were issued with a Certificate of Settlement, a written statement from the parish undertaking to take them back, or pay any other parish for taking care of them. An act of 1697 barred strangers from entering a parish

26 Date stone on the Town Bridge at the end of West Street.

27 Ironwell Lane, once the coach road from Rochford to London.

28 The old cannon was placed outside the post office to prevent vehicles damaging the walls.

29 The Post Office in North Street before the motor car.

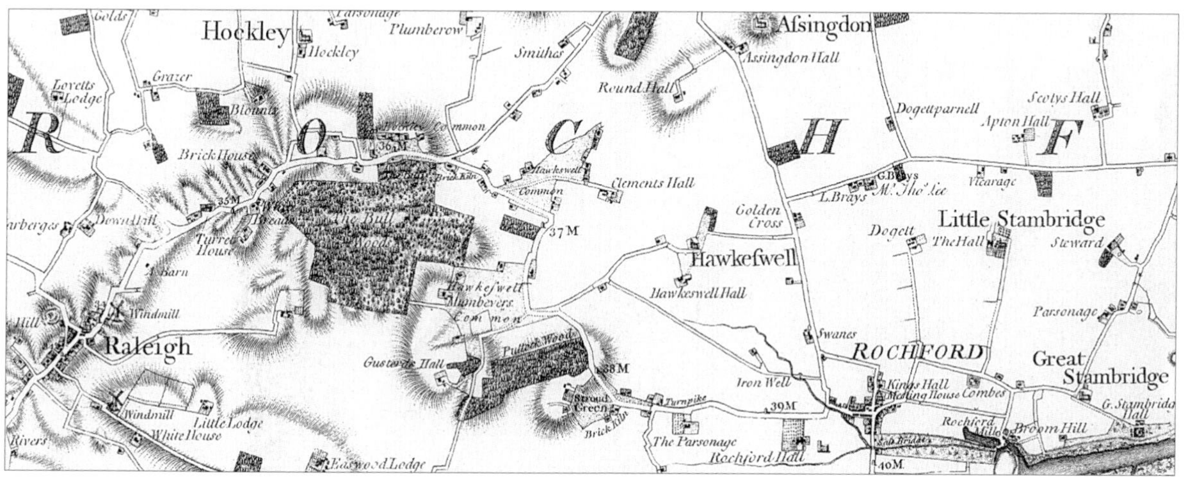

30 Chapman and André's map showing the Rochford turnpike near Cherry Orchard Lane, 1777.

unless they had a certificate. All the important documents were kept in the church in the parish chest, which had three locks and could only be opened when all three key holders were present. Vagrants were dealt with very harshly, penalties ranging from whipping to hanging. Those incapable of working were issued with a licence to beg in a designated area.

One of the most neglected of the parish's responsibility was the roads, which were in most cases no more than dirt tracks. At the centre of Rochford, four main roads radiate like the points of a compass. South Street crossed the ford and carried on to the Priory at Prittlewell. The three-arched brick Salt Bridge was built over the ford about the same time that the Town Bridge was built at the end of West Street in 1777. This road went through Ironwell Lane, so named because of the well which was situated where the railway bridge in the lane is now, then made its way to Hockley and on to Rayleigh and Shenfield. The present Hall Road was constructed in the latter part of the 18th century; prior to its construction the road from Hawkwell to Rochford passed behind the Hall. It was changed to its present position by Sir Tylney Long in 1784.

North Street led to Ashingdon and across the ferry to North Fambridge, Maldon and Chelmsford. East Street took the traveller through Stambridge to Creeksea and the ferry there. Huge posts were placed along the edge of the muddy, furrowed roads to shield pedestrians from passing carts. Sometimes cannon were hammered into the ground to protect property; one of these can still be seen outside the post office.

According to Benton, the lack of drainage contributed to the terrible outbreaks of malaria and ague amongst the inhabitants. Many farmers refused to complain about the state of the roads for fear that improvements would mean an increase in their rents. Turnpike Trusts eventually set up toll roads or turnpikes as commercial undertakings. The first Turnpike Act of 1706 decreed that certain roads could be closed, gates erected and tolls charged by private companies. Chapman and André's map of 1777 shows that the Rochford turnpike gate was situated on Hall Road, near Cherry Orchard Lane. The toll road from Rochford through Rayleigh to Shenfield was 21 miles in length. Charges to use it ranged from 2s. 6d. for a carriage to 3d. for a score of sheep or lambs. Maintenance of the

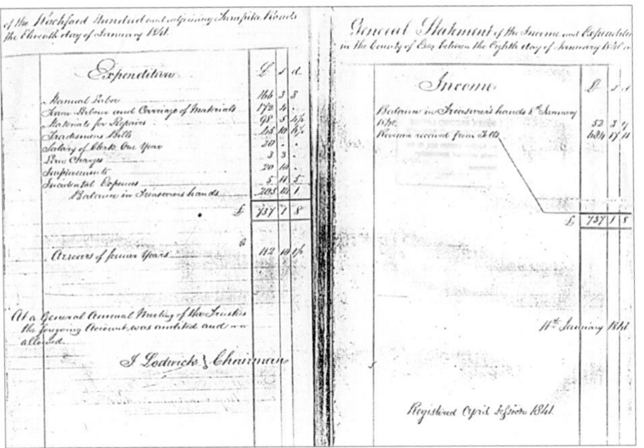

General Statement of the Income and Expenditure of the Rochford Hundred and adjoining Turnpike Roads in the County of Essex between the Eighth day of January 1840 and the Eleventh day of January 1841.

Expenditure	£	s	d
Manual Labor	166	3	8
Team Labour and Carriage of Materials	172	4	.
Materials for Repairs	98	5	4½
Tradesmens Bills	[illegible]	10	[illegible]
Salary of Clerk One Year	20	.	.
Law Charges	3	3	.
Improvements	20	10	.
Incidental Expenses	5	14	5
Balance in Treasurers hands	205	10	1
£	737	7	8
Arrears of former Years	112	10	1½

At a General Annual Meeting of the Trustees the foregoing Account was audited and allowed.

J. Lodwick } Chairman

Income	£	s	d
Balance in Treasurers hands 8th January 1840	52	3	9
Revenue received from Tolls	684	17	11
£	737	1	8

11th January 1841

Registered April Sessions 1841

31 Statement of income from the Turnpike Trust in 1841.

roads was the responsibility of the Turnpike Trust. By 1820 the Reverend William Benson Ramsden was treasurer of the Hockley gate; the balance of accounts showed a little over £120. Tolls were paid at a small hut close to Turnpike Cottages by Cherry Orchard Lane (these were pulled down in 1964) but it became common practice for those who knew the road to drive off the highway just before the tollgate, go over the fields and rejoin the road again just past the next gate to avoid paying the fees.

As a result of the improvement of the roads, the journey by stagecoach became more comfortable and therefore more popular. First introduced from Kocin in Hungary, they had been conveying passengers and goods since the 16th century; later they carried the mail as well. The average speed was ten miles per hour.

Smuggling was rife in Rochford and surrounding districts. Many of the village churches provided a secure and popular hiding place for contraband and Rochford's St Andrew's was no exception. According to Benton, 'gin, Hollands and dollops of tea' were hidden in the tower. Under the pulpit was a secret cavity called the Magazine, where the smugglers hid their shot and powder. In

32 Weir Pond Road, showing the Customs House on the left.

33 Lukers Brewery, used by Cramphorn's as storage, and by a car breaker, was at the rear of the old Customs House.

an article in the *Southend Times* of 1928, Mr James Moss tells how his father was one of Rochford's smuggling fraternity. He used to run the local 'Ghost Bus'. Mr Moss would bind its wheels with thick cloth and cover the horses' hooves with sponge so that he could drive the ghost bus silently through the lanes to Stambridge, where he would meet the boat and collect the goods. The article also tells of daring smuggler Peter Wright, who was busy hiding a huge bale of tobacco under a great earth mound when the customs men arrived on the scene. One of them plunged a long spear into the bale and when it was pulled out the tip smelt of tobacco. Peter was in trouble, transportation being the usual punishment for those caught. The Custom House was situated in Weir Pond Road.

A newspaper article printed in 1934 tells of the legend of the man who, after betraying some of the local smugglers in 1834, suddenly disappeared. A hundred years later, Waterworks men, digging in a ditch, found the well-preserved body of a man, thought to be that of the betrayer.

Five

Churches and Chapels

The small groups of nonconformists who set up their own meeting places had to contend with the dreaded Bishop Bonner, who was very active in searching out those who would not conform to the teaching of the established church. John Simson from Great Wigborough was 'put to the flames' for his protestant convictions close to Rochford Market Place in 1555. A plaque to his memory is on the wall of Market Alley.

34 The plaque in memory of John Simson.

Congregationalists

Despite the persecution, dissenters continued to hold their own services. Rochford's first dissenters were the Congregationalists, who held their meetings at Rochford Hall. In order not to interfere with the service in St Andrew's, the nonconformists, led by Robert Wright, held their meetings at eight o'clock in the evening, after the service at the parish church. The setting up of this new church caused considerable disquiet in the community. Eventually the Queen was informed that dissenters were rife in Essex and practising in the home of Lord Rich. Robert Wright was accused of calling followers of the Book of Common Prayer 'dumb dogs' and of luring the congregation away from the services at St Andrew's, and was sent to the notorious Fleet Prison in London. Lord Rich went to Marshalsea Prison. Both were eventually released. Congregationalism continued in secret until the Toleration Act of 1689 gave limited freedom to nonconformists.

The Congregational Chapel in North Street was opened in 1741 and was the only nonconformist church in Rochford until the end of the 18th century. The chapel was about half the size of the present church and the dissenters had their own burial ground at the rear. In 1750 a Mr Wallman of Southchurch presented the Minister's house, in 1808 a school was opened and in 1838 the chapel was enlarged at a cost of £600. Mr Ebenezer Temple was persuaded to become pastor of the chapel and, despite his ill health, he worked

35 Rochford church.

36 The one brass in St Andrew's Church, Rochford.

tirelessly for the people of Rochford and the surrounding area. Ebenezer died in 1841 in London. At his request his body was brought back to Rochford and all the shops in the town closed as a mark of respect for this much admired man. A tablet to him can be seen in the church. There is also a tablet to Mr Thomas Scott, who died in 1853 aged 65. He drove the mail coach from Rochford to Southend and Great Wakering for many years. Three children of the important Tabor family are remembered by a memorial in the church.

Methodists

There have been Methodists in Rochford since 1822; they used premises in Market Alley rented from George Whipps of Little Stambridge. Later they rented a small hall in North Street for

37 The Wesleyan Church, North Street.

£1 a year, on a 29-year lease. When it was due for renewal the new lease stated that the owner was able to dismantle the building at any time without notice. Not happy with this arrangement, the trustees decided to build a new chapel. Southend man George Baxter, renowned for building chapels, purchased one-third of an acre in North Street from the Board of Guardians of the Rochford Union for £180. The cost of building was £800, much of which was met by Mr Baxter, who had amassed a fortune in the oyster and winkle industry. The Wesleyans raised part of the money themselves by renting out the pews at 9d. a quarter, or 2s. 6d. for a family of four. Mr Baxter lent the money to buy a harmonium. In 1852 a certificate of public worship was issued and later the same year the chapel was registered for marriages. The old building was made into four cottages. In 1885 a meeting was called to plan the formation of a Sunday School and a new school was built. Children were encouraged to help. If they saved 2s. 6d. they were allowed to lay a brick and receive a commemorative card. The school was opened by Mrs Shelly in 1898. By 1930, thanks to a generous gift from Mr Beehag and Mr Price, an extension costing £222 was made to the schoolroom. The bricks and cement were donated by P. and H. Cottis in memory of their parents. During the war the room was used as a classroom for the primary school children from the Council School.

Peculiar People

James Banyard was born in 1800 in a small cottage in Barrack Lane. His father was

38 Part of the Rochford Barracks adjoining the *Marlborough Head*.

39 Union Lane; it was here that James Banyard held his early meetings.

ploughman at Rochford Hall. As a young man he was by trade a shoemaker and by inclination a troublemaker. He and his friend William Lazell were well known locally for their lawless way of life, smuggling, poaching and generally causing trouble. James spent his free time in rowdy public houses, singing bawdy songs and scoffing at religion. One day, after losing all his money at the Paglesham fair, he promised his wife that he would reform and began to attend the Wesley Chapel. There he met London hat block maker William Bridges. Listening to him changed James' life and he became a regular worshipper at the church. Eventually he became a preacher himself and often took the service at the church in North Street. After hearing the doctrine of a minister named Atkins, who preached a less formal kind of religion favouring life and liberty, James formed his own group in West Street. Thanks to the harassment and the damage done to the property by jeering locals, the landlord asked him to leave, and he moved to a cottage in Union Lane.

James was an ugly man with a voice of thunder and great charisma, and his devotees rapidly grew in number, and soon the cottage in Union Lane became too cramped. Other, larger premises had to be found. By this time James had married again, this time to Judith Knapping who was quite well off, and with her money they were able to move to a hall in North Street. The group named themselves 'The Peculiar People'. The name was taken from chapter 14 of the Old Testament Book of Deuteronomy, which said 'The Lord hath chosen thee to be a Peculiar People unto himself'. The sect denounced doctors, believing in faith healing. Miracles achieved through prayer include a woman who was cured of

40 Banyard's grave in Rochford churchyard.

lockjaw; blind people regained their sight, the dumb regained their speech, and the lame walked again. Four children of Peculiar People died through lack of medical help. Their deaths were reported to the Union but no proceedings were taken against the parents. People came from miles around to hear James preach and the Peculiars, or Banyardites, set up chapels all over Essex. James was ordained their first bishop. Sadly, one of his children became very ill and despite all his principles he called for a doctor. As this was against the teaching of the church he was not allowed to remain a bishop but he continued to preach at Rochford until his death in 1863. His grave is in Rochford churchyard.

Baptists

The Baptists held their meetings in a tiny room at a cottage in South Street. Cryer tells us that it was pulled down and rebuilt with stone from Little Stambridge church when that was demolished in 1891. The house was called Zion Villa. Strictly speaking they were named the Hyper Baptists, but they had no regular preacher. Later a Baptist church meeting was held in Warwick Drive.

Six

The Market Town

Rochford has always been mainly a farming community; every farm had a few cottages for its workers but the rest of the houses and shops were clustered around the four main roads that met at the Market Square. The market was first granted in 1264 along with a fair to be held on Easter Tuesday and the Wednesday after 29 September for 'toys, pedlery, tailors and gloves and goods'. It closed down sometime during the early 18th century and stayed closed for several years, but it was later reopened by John Harriott who lived at Broomhills. In his book *Struggles through Life*, he said there was no other market for 20 miles and to open one would be of great benefit to the town and surrounding villages. Once the market was established he persuaded some of the farmers to meet and dine at the *New Ship* each market day and organised them into a group whose aim was to keep law and order. The Rochford Hundred Association Against Murderers, Felons and Thieves etc. was formed, its aim being to

41 Broomhills, once the home of John Harriott.

42 The blue plaque at Broomhills presented by Rochford Historical Society.

43 North Street. The *Old Ship* on the right was recorded as an inn as early as 1670.

suppress crime. The membership fee was 10s.6d. The association met all reasonable expenses caused by the apprehending and prosecuting of offenders. The reward for bringing to justice a murderer, housebreaker, or anyone setting fire to a barn or stack, or stealing or maliciously killing a member's horse was £10. Catching a highwayman, footpad, poacher or anyone maiming a sheep, ox, bull or cow was worth £5.

The market proved to be a great success and the Square would be packed with stalls, cattle pens, acrobats, wandering players and musicians. The *Old Ship* was a favourite with the fairground folk, and the landlord had several hooks fixed to the outside wall where performing bears could be tethered while their owners went inside. The farmers frequented the ancient *Marlborough Head*, considered a rough place. A group of farmers would arrive with a hen and her clutch of eggs and not leave until all the eggs were hatched. The Earl of Mornington presented the Market Hall for the benefit of the parish and it was erected in the Square in 1707. It possibly stood on the site of an earlier building and was of wood and plaster with a tiled roof. A flimsy wooden

44 Pewter pub measure made for the *Old Ship*.

45 One-gallon stone flagon used for beer or spirits made for the *Old Ship*.

construction was added to the roof to hold the bell. On one side, under a gable, was a large clock. The ground floor was a series of open arches, with an area for pigs which was later used as a barber's shop and a shelter for the local fire engine. On the second floor was a spacious loft used for storing and weighing wool. Later this housed poles and the general gear used in setting up the stalls for the markets and fairs. There was also a small compartment on the ground floor called 'the cage' where disorderly persons were confined while they waited to be taken to the magistrates. One drunk, recovering from the night before in the town lockup, must have sobered up quite quickly when he realised that someone was taking pot shots at the cage. He managed to dodge the bullets by lying on the floor and finally emerged shaken but unhurt. The shots had been fired by some of the Rochford Volunteers who, having little to do, decided to try a little target practice on the Market Hall, unaware that anyone was inside. The Market House became derelict and had to be pulled down in 1861. The bell was transferred to the new Corn Exchange.

An early census shows that in 1801 there were 180 dwelling houses in Rochford, and 1,228 people. This number included all those living at the Hall. The only water available, even at the Hall, was from the river or from wells. Rochford was fortunate in having several reliable wells in the town, including one in Ironwell Lane; some say this was named after the hard water it contained, but Arthur Stephenson remembers that the well was situated where the railway bridge in the lane is now and was so named because it was made of iron instead of the more usual brick. There was another in the house on the corner of Ironwell Lane and Ashingdon Road which has belonged to the Sparrow family for many years; the well is still in the garden. There was another in Watts Lane, several in North Street, one near the *White Horse*, and one in the yard at the back of the *Golden Lion* (formerly known as the *Red Lion*) which served the residents of North Street. Some properties had more than one well, one house in South Street having five. A pump at the *Horse and Groom* was used by the people in Watt's Lane, one in North

46 Drawing of the Market Hall showing the bell tower and the clock. The Market House became derelict and was pulled down in 1861.

Street was called Molly Thompson's pump and there were several others, but the main and most loved pump was the one built in the Market Square. The fine pump was erected in 1820 and paid for by public subscription. The well was 100 feet deep and over seven feet across at the top and 25 feet across at the bottom. The great iron pump was about eight feet high and had a huge curved handle. Written on the side was 'erected by voluntary subscription 1820'. It stood close to the Market House, opposite the saddler's shop. Anyone

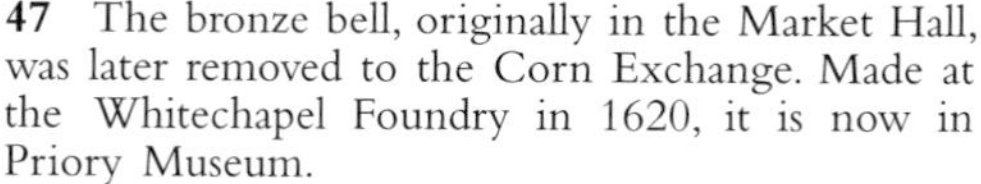

47 The bronze bell, originally in the Market Hall, was later removed to the Corn Exchange. Made at the Whitechapel Foundry in 1620, it is now in Priory Museum.

Parish ~~or Township~~ of Rochford	~~Ecclesiastical District~~ of The See of Rochester		~~City or Borough~~ of			
Houses	Name of Street, Place, or Road, and Name or No. of House	Name and Surname of each Person who abode in the house, on the Night of the 30th March, 1851	Relation to Head of Family	Condition	Age of Males	Age of Females
		James Simpson	Son		8	
		Michael Do	Son		6	
		Jacob Do	Son		4	
11	North Street	Eliza Coe	Head	W		24
		Charles Do	Son		4	
		Emma Do	Daur			2
		George Watts	Brother	U	16	
12		Frederick Johnson	Head	Mar	23	
		Harriet Do	Wife	Mar		21
		William Do	Son		11 m	
13	North Street Police Station	Henry Flood	Head	Mar	40	
		Marian Do	Wife	Mar		35
		John C. H. Do	Son		10	
14	North Street	James Haywards	Head	Mar	47	
		Mary Do	Wife	Mar		41
		Sarah Do	Daur			12
		Ellen Do	Daur			10
		George Do	Son		7	
		Alfred Fowkes	Nephew		2	
I 3 U B			Total of Persons		12	7

48 Part of the 1851 census showing the people living in North Street.

was free to help themselves. After a while the pump was bought by Sam Steward, who employed a man to act as caretaker. After it could no longer cope with the demand, its use had to be restricted to twice a day and a charge was made. A bucketful of water now cost one farthing. The enterprising postmaster Mr Garood had a well dug in his garden in Back Lane. He mounted a huge barrel on a horse-drawn cart and paid someone to take it round the town selling water at a farthing a bucketful.

Most people ran some kind of business from their home, the wife often setting up a business in the front room, dress or bonnet making, or

49 The *Horse and Groom* was once in the parish of Eastwood.

50 Inside the *Golden Lion*.

a laundry or alehouse. There were dozens of cottages where beer was sold, since it was easy and cheap to make and more hygienic than most of the water available at the time. Some of the shops doubled as inns. The *Prince of Wales* in North Street was run by J.&G.Searles, and was also a family butcher's shop with an abattoir at the back.

The main meeting place for men was the inn, and Rochford had its fair share of them. The *Old Ship* was built around 1600 has mostly been used as an inn, although at one time there was a butcher's shop in the yard owned by a young man named Thomas Fairhead, who was engaged to Mary Waters, the landlord's daughter. Thomas and his friend Henry Gilliott, a shepherd from Prittlewell, were hanged at Moulsham in Chelmsford in 1820 for sheep and cattle stealing, the last men in England to be hanged for this offence. Both were under twenty years old and, soon after the hanging, Mary Waters died of a broken heart. Most were coaching inns. The *King's Head*, known as the *Blue Boar* until around 1793, was one of the main stops. Coaches would leave the Square and travel to Rayleigh, Billericay and on to Shenfield. Later a stagecoach and a diligence, a continental-style coach, made the journey three times a week, through Ironwell Lane and on to London. The fare was eight shillings. Coaching inns had stabling facilities and an ostler and a blacksmith to attend to the horses. The old

51 The Town Pump stood in the Square from 1820 to 1902.

52 The water cart was once a popular sight in the town.

53 The *Prince of Wales*, in North Street, where the pet shop is now.

blacksmith's forge and stables at the rear of the *King's Head* were only finally demolished in 2001 to make way for a private house. Coaches left the *Rose and Crown* for London three times a week, at 7a.m. in the summer and 8a.m. in the winter; a coach left the *Vernon's Head* in West Street at 5 o'clock each morning except Sunday, travelling through Rayleigh, Billericay, Brentwood and Romford and on to the *Blue Boar* in Aldgate. The average speed was ten miles and hour, with frequent stops to change horses. Despite the improvements in the roads, journeys by coach were long and uncomfortable.

An ancient and important local industry was brick making, which started in Roman times. Given their weight it was easier to make the bricks on site than transport them. They were fashioned from clay and fired in a hole in the ground. Being expensive, they were used only in the houses of the rich until the middle of the 16th century.

Several small brickmaking companies were later set up but there were two main brickfields in the town: one in Tinker's Lane by Purdey's Farm on the bank of the river near Stambridge Mill, was owned by Mr Lamb of Rayleigh; the other in Cherry Orchard Lane, where

ROCHFORD, ESSEX.

Particulars and Conditions of Sale of

FREEHOLD PROPERTY

COMPRISING

A VALUABLE FREE BEER-HOUSE,

Known as the "PRINCE OF WALES," and

A FREEHOLD COTTAGE,

Situate in North Street;

TWO FREEHOLD HOUSES,

Situate in East Street; and a Small

LEASEHOLD PROPERTY,

Situate in North Street; consisting of the Erections of

THREE COTTAGES & GARDEN GROUND,

WHICH WILL BE SOLD BY AUCTION, BY

MR. T. W. OFFIN

By direction of the Trustees of the Will of Mr. William Clark, deceased,

AT THE "KING'S HEAD INN," ROCHFORD,

ON THURSDAY, MAY 15th, 1884,

AT 4 O'CLOCK IN THE AFTERNOON,

IN FOUR LOTS.

Solicitors:

MESSRS. GEO: WOOD & SON,
Rochford, and 7, New Broad Street,
London, E.C.

54 Bill of sale for the *Prince of Wales*.

55 The old forge at the rear of the *King's Head* in Back Lane.

bricks known as Essex Reds were made by the Milton Hall Brick Company. They also had a site in Star Lane. Rochford was an ideal place for the industry: the clay soil, known as brick earth, was excellent for brick making, and transport was easy with the River Crouch nearby. Bricks from Rochford were loaded onto specially made barges or 'brickies'. Smaller and more roughly built than the traditional barge, they carried around 30,000 bricks. To take them to London was a day's work for a four-man loading gang. On the return trips the boats would carry chalk and fuel: the chalk was an important ingredient in the making of bricks; the fuel was mostly ash and household waste from London which would be brought up the river and unloaded on the wharf at Broomhills.

Also on the river was the mill. Domesday Book records one windmill in Rochford and there have been several others since then, but

56 The brickfields in Cherry Orchard Lane.

there is some doubt as to their whereabouts. We know there was one in Stambridge in 1254, when Henry III granted Phillip Basset the Manor of Stambridge, and the church, millpond, marshes and woods. In 1552 it is recorded in the church minutes that 'the church wardens mended the highwaye leading to the mylle and to the market for £3 8s. 2d.' The tidemill at Stambridge has been there since 1710; by 1800 it was run by steam. The mill was taken over by John Kemp and his brother Robert in 1809. The sale included barns, kiln, granary, wharf, water wheel, tide gates, swing bridge as well as a post mill with going gears. In his will dated 1826 builder John Kemp bequeathed his tools and all his trade implements to his son John. The executors, Thomas Merrifield, brewer, and William Quy, cabinet maker, were to sell all his goods and chattels, all his properties and securities, and divide the money equally among his six children. £25 was to be given to his grandson James when he reached 14 years of age so that he could be apprenticed. The will was signed with Mr Kemp's seal and 'X' his mark.

In 1835 Tabor and Rankin took over the mill, having been granted a lease of 21 years at an annual rent of £250. Mr Rankin spent nearly £800 enlarging the pool and repainting the mill and the mill house. The 1841 census mentions the Tabors as millers and brewers. The wharf beside the mill could hold several barges; mill owner Mr Rankin owned two of them, the *Lord Robert* and the *Joy*.

The ancient craft of potash making was carried out in various parts of the hundred. Potash was used in bleaching, for dying, and for soap making; it was also used by glassmakers. Originally it was produced by burning vegetables in big iron pots. Many of the farmers made their own potash, which they used as a fertiliser. Potash was made commercially in Rochford by Barnabas

57 Barges at Stambridge Mill.

58 The Square. The large house on the left is Connaught House.

Townsend at his premises at the end of North Street called the Potash. Wood, ash and water were put into a large tub and then percolated. Red Essex potash was made by dipping wheat straw into the vat and burning it; it took 20 loads of straw to make one hogshead of potash. When all the goodness had been taken out the ash that remained was called ashlip. This was used as manure, and cost around ten shillings for 40 bushels. The wood for these processes was gathered from Potash Wood. The Potash closed around 1860.

Most of the trades employed casual labour and work was fairly easy to come by in the summer, but at times there were dozens of itinerants wandering around the country looking for work. The *Crown* (now the *Rose and Crown*) was nicknamed the 'Pad and Can', because of the number of vagrants and tramps who spent the night in a shed at the rear of the property.

Opposite the *Crown* was a piece of land measuring half a rood, which was included in Joslyns Charity and was let in 1810 for £20 on a 60-year lease to Thomas Hayward, at a yearly rent of £1 1s. The tenant had the right to remove any building, including the two cottages on the land, at the end of the lease. The Joslyns

59 The Hollies.

Charity originated in 1806 with Thomas Joslyn's will. It also owns nine acres, three roods and 19 poles of land given by an unknown donor in 1786, which consisted of a boarded cottage called the Pest House, on arable land on part of Rochford Common, and 5 acres and 4 poles on the north side of Ironwell Lane.

Some of the more wealthy men built grand houses around this time. The Georgian-style Connaught House, on the west side of the Square, was built around 1780 by Irishman Mr Collis with his winnings from a lottery. It later became part of the hospital. It was at one time the home of Mr Halsey, shipping manager of the Hudson Bay Fur Company, and at another by John Comport, who was clerk to the workhouse, and then by land agent and auctioneer William Gregson. His brother Frederick lived in 'The Lavenders'. The Lavenders, built without foundations and situated near the bottom of West Street, was described in 1926 when it was auctioned as a delightful, picturesque, old-fashioned timber and brick built residence with 5 bedrooms, a maid's bedroom, large lounge, kitchen with range and dresser, scullery, housekeeper's store, small conservatory, nice garden, 3 timber built tenements, two tenements producing a rental of £58 8s. 8d. with the landlord paying all outgoings. It was sold prior to the auction to the Board of Guardians of the Rochford Union for £1,750, and has since been pulled down to make way for new housing. Further up West Street is the Hollies, a large Georgian-fronted house which belonged to George Wood the solicitor, and has in its time been the rates office and the post office; during the war the kitchen was used to cook meals for the needy.

Acacia House at the end of East Street was built in 1882 by Thomas Quy, the ironmonger,

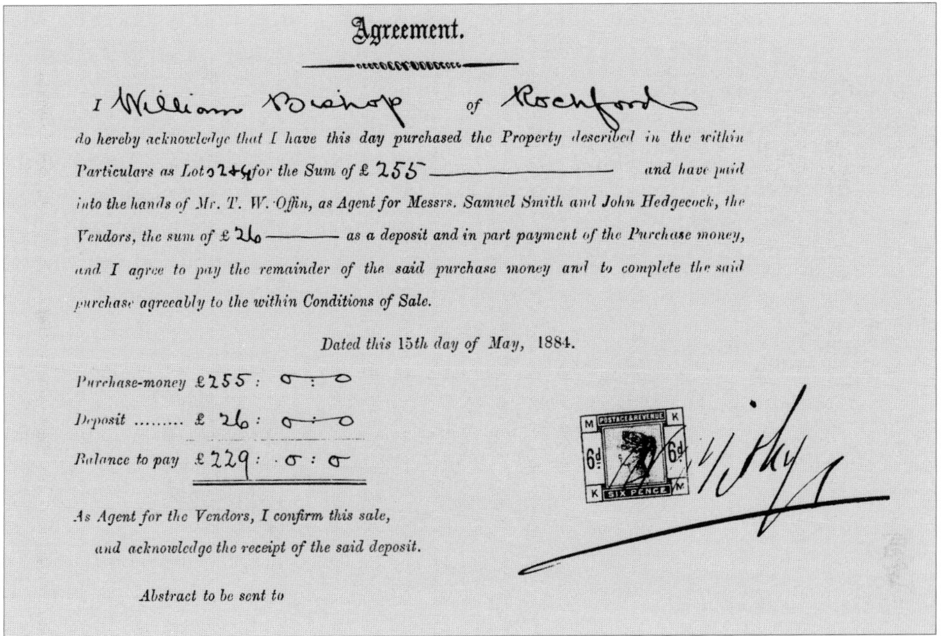

Agreement.

I William Bishop of Rochford

do hereby acknowledge that I have this day purchased the Property described in the within Particulars as Lots 2+4 for the Sum of £ 255 and have paid into the hands of Mr. T. W. Offin, as Agent for Messrs. Samuel Smith and John Hedgecock, the Vendors, the sum of £ 26 as a deposit and in part payment of the Purchase money, and I agree to pay the remainder of the said purchase money and to complete the said purchase agreeably to the within Conditions of Sale.

Dated this 15th day of May, 1884.

Purchase-money £255 : 0 : 0

Deposit .... £ 26 : 0 : 0

Balance to pay £229 : 0 : 0

As Agent for the Vendors, I confirm this sale, and acknowledge the receipt of the said deposit.

Abstract to be sent to

60-1 An agreement to pay £225 for the purchase of Acacia House and land included in the sale.

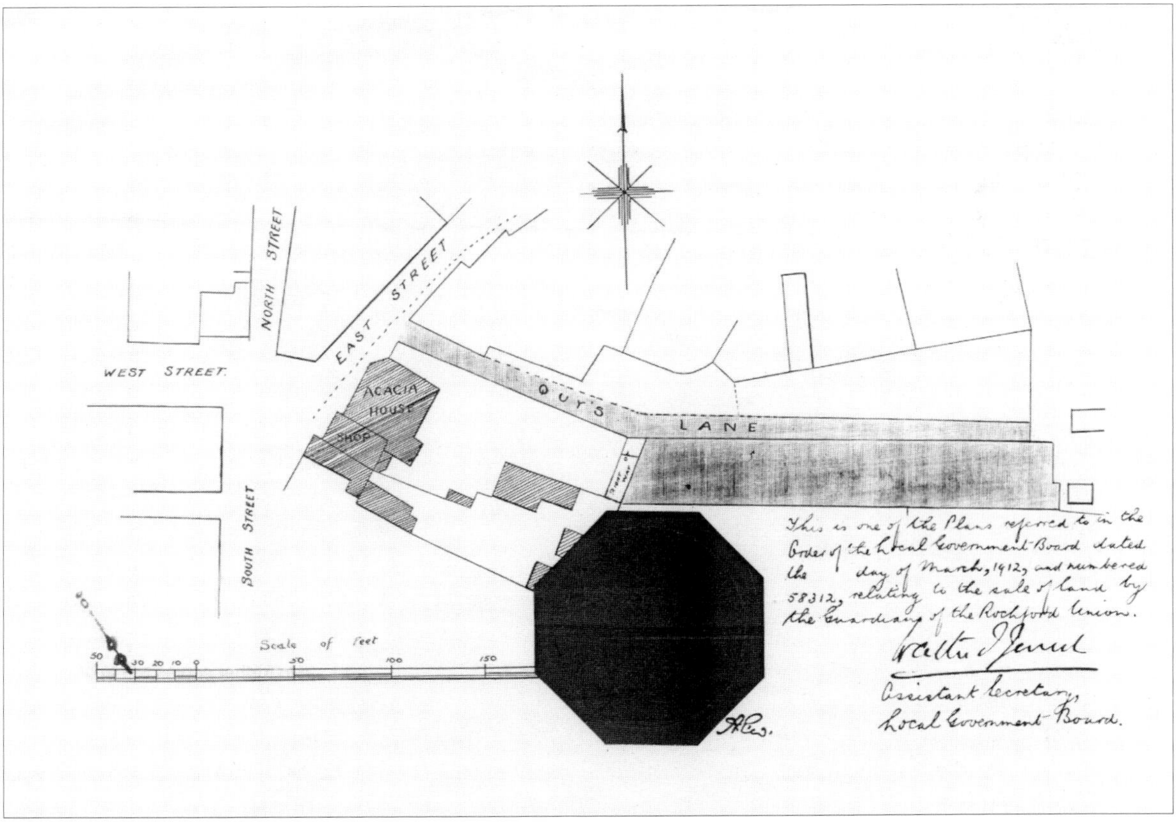

NORTH STREET

EAST STREET

WEST STREET

ACACIA HOUSE

SHOP

GUY'S LANE

SOUTH STREET

Scale of Feet

50 30 20 10 0 50 100 150

This is one of the Plans referred to in the Order of the Local Government Board dated the day of March, 1912, and numbered 58312, relating to the sale of land by the Guardians of the Rochford Union.

Walter Jerred

Assistant Secretary, Local Government Board.

for his occupation. It has had several changes of ownership and use. At one time it was converted to a gym, later it was used to house a hundred people from the Union at Greenwich, and in 1904 it was listed as the Receiving House for children from the workhouse, the matron being Mrs Hart. By the '30s it had become a night nurses' home. Miss Potter's trustees auctioned the property in 1907, when it was advertised as Acacia Lodge, once owned by Messrs Quy Bros, together with a strip of land occupied by Mr Boatman. The property was divided into four lots: Lot 1, the house with eight bedrooms, the ironmonger's shop and premises; Lot 2 was land with buildings thereon; Lot 3 was garden land, a strip alongside Quy's land; Lot 4 was land stretching from the rear of the house as far as the gas works. The Guardians

62 Acacia House.

63 South Street, once called the High Street. The first house on the left was the Manse.

of the Poor purchased the land and premises and agreed to let Mr Quy take over the latter until 1908 at a yearly rent of £15. The shop and the two rooms above were used by him as an ironmonger's shop. In 1911 Mr Boatman offered to buy the land at the rear of the house known as Acacia House Garden Ground for £45 and Mr Rankin mooted that this should be agreed upon. Mr Jackson proposed, and Mr Tabor seconded the proposal that it should be sold for £50 with the stipulation that only greenhouses or conservatories should be built there. The motion was carried by nine votes to four.

Next to Acacia House, the first house in South Street was the Manse, home to the minister of the Congregational church; next was Roche House, for years the home of the doctor. Part of Cromwell House next door was used as a draper's shop. All these properties from Acacia House to the Red House, and later the Old House, were taken over by the council, and are now used as council offices.

Seven

Law and Order

By the end of the 18th century, fear of a French invasion had forced Parliament to organise a supplementary Militia and Provisional Cavalry, a sort of Territorial Army, to stop Napoleon's troops who might land on the Essex coast. Each Hundred was told to raise a group of Volunteers. The Rochford Overseers Records of 1779-1809 include a letter to the overseers of Rochford and Raweth and Little Stambridge telling them they are to 'call together all principal members of the parish vestry and put a notice in writing on the vestry door to raise a certain number of men for service in his Majesty's army and navy'. It is dated 13 December 1796. The constable of Rochford was required 'to make true and correct returns. You are to require the assistance of the churchwardens, overseers and such other intelligent inhabitants of the parish that will be willing to lend their aid towards this essential service.'

The constable was ordered to call a vestry meeting on Monday 25 July to complete the returns. One fit and proper person was to be nominated to take the chair of superintendent and carry out such measures as were necessary to be taken for the defence of the county.

SCHEDUIE No. 1.

FORM of the Paper to be given in shewing the Live and Dead Stock of th Parish of *Rochford* in the County of Essex.

NAMES.	Live Stock. Oxen	Cows	Young Cattle and Colts	Sheep and Goats	Pigs	Horses. Riding	Draft	Waggons	Carts	Average Amount of Dead Stock. Wheat, Quarters of	Oats, Quarters of	Barley, Quarters of	Beans and Pease, Quarters of	Hay, Loads of	Straw, Loads of	Potatoes, Sacks of	Flour or other Meal. Quarters of	Sacks of	Malt, Quarters of	Blank Columns for any Articles of local Produce not herein specified. Wheat	Beans	Barley	Oats		
Revd Mr Wise		2	2		13	2	4	1	1					18						32	4	6	4		[illegible]
[illegible] Carr		5	6	590	—	4	2	2	2					30						10	—	24			
Mr Wright	29	8	2 3	220	109	3	16	3	5					100						100	62	20	60		
Mr Barrington																				4	3				
Robt Evans		4		30	24		3		1					10											
Wm Saward		14	6	15	13		5	2	3	14				20						30	28	4	12		
Mr Townsend		4		—	7	1	4	4	4					6						5	4	—	3		
Mr [illegible]			7		11									4						11	4		2		5 [illegible]
Mrs [illegible]					2		1		1																
Miss [illegible]							1		1									12							
Mr Water						1			1					8											
[illegible] Bright		1			24	1	3	1	1	20	10								100	6	—	—	—		12 [illegible]
Mr [illegible] Thorne		9		100	17	1	2	2	6					20						10	7	7		302	13 [illegible]
Wm Cook																		10							
E Appleton																		12							
Mr Johnson					2	1			1																
Jas Digby						1			1																

Should this Sheet not be sufficient to contain the above Return, add one or more Sheets of plain Paper at Bottom.

64 Militia returns: the Secretary of State demanded exact details of all people, stock and local produce.

65 Members of the Rochford Police Division around 1873.

Names of persons willing to serve as officers and pioneers should be returned at a meeting in the *King's Head* on Tuesday 26 July at 10 o'clock, in order that an exact account of persons, livestock, horses, the amount of dead stock, flour, meal and other local product should be reported to the Lord Lieutenant and then to the Secretary of State. This was signed by order of J. Parker, Clerk of the general meeting. In 1803 Overseers Thomas Haywood and R. Salmon were fined £20 for not raising enough men. The bakers of Rochford said that in a case of invasion they would faithfully promise to bake and deliver such quantities of good wholesome loaves of three or four pounds whenever required to do so, and be afterwards paid for such loaves at such rates as considered to be suitable by the magistrate appointed for the purpose. J. Barrington was churchwarden and Edward Cooling and John Wade constables.

The Rochford district raised several platoons of Volunteers. Every company of 50 men had a captain, who received 5s. per day; non-commissioned officers were paid a shilling a day. John Asplin of Wakering recruited a group of cavalry volunteers. John Barrington was captain of the Rochford contingent, which met on Hawkwell Common. The uniform was a jacket and pantaloons. The cavalry wore half boots and a green feather in their caps; the infantry wore black gaiters and white feathers in their leather caps. Rev. Wise was appointed Captain Pioneer, and it was his duty to direct the people in their retreat whenever the government decided. An inventory at the time lists 70 private and two public ovens, 60 oxen, 49 cows, 754 sheep and goats, 150 pigs, 22 riding horses, 71 draft horses,

66 The *Anne Boleyn* took over from the *Three Ashes.*

16 waggons and 22 carts in Rochford. The Rochford Volunteers were renowned for their practical jokes, surrounding the windmill in Barling one day with one of the officers climbing up onto the sail for a dare and clinging there precariously while the sails continued to rotate.

Benton writes that the whole country was in a state of disorder at this time, vagabonds and pilfering depredators abounding; even the men of wealth were defiant of the law. The belief in witchcraft was very strong in the area. Rochford Hall had a rather unruly ghost who amused himself by throwing boots and shoes at men's heads and many an old woman accused of being a witch was tied to the ducking stool and plunged into the water at the Bobbing Pond. Mrs West of Stambridge Road was accused of putting curses upon those who crossed her. She was said to use the juice of the poppies she grew in her garden to feed her imps and she and her husband were swum in the river: in front of a large crowed they were tied by a rope to a boat. Mr West nearly drowned and was declared innocent; Mrs West floated like a cork and was deemed to be a witch. Canewdon was and still is connected with witchcraft, there being six witches in the village always. One young girl was burnt at the stake in the churchyard and it is said that her ghost still haunts the *Anchor.* The White Witches, or wise women, would dispense herbal remedies

THE

ROCHFORD TOWN ESTATE

Is within two miles of Southend-on-Sea High Street, about $1\frac{1}{2}$ miles of Prittlewell, Victoria Avenue, and the New Electric Tramway, Abuts on the Main Roads

From SOUTHEND via PRITTLEWELL and SUTTON,

WITHIN

TEN MINUTES OF ROCHFORD STATION, G.E. RAILWAY,

AND

Close to the Historic Old Hall and Church,

IN THE

CENTRE OF CHARMINGLY PICTURESQUE COUNTRY.

FOR

Those desiring Quietude and Repose,

AND TO BE

YET WITHIN EASY REACH OF LONDON,

THIS ESTATE

Affords an Excellent Opportunity.

WATER MAINS are to be laid forthwith by the Rural District Council in the Sutton Road, which passes the Estate.

THE LAND CO., 68, Cheapside, E.C.

Solicitors :—Messrs. LAYTONS, 29, Budge Row, E.C.

67 Rochford Town Estate—sale notice.

and strange cures; doctors resorted to bleeding, purging and electuaries; the blacksmith would often officiate at the pulling of teeth. Benton goes on to say that the clergy were incompetent and failed to carry out their duties. He tells of one vicar who turned the parsonage into a granary and drove his pigs to market dressed in velvet breeches and a blue frock coat and never failed to stop at the *Three Ashes*.

On the road from the *Three Ashes* to Barling was a farm named Goal Farm, which dates back to the 15th century and was possibly a manorial Court House; nearby was a field called Gallows Acre, where the gallows stood on a hill 'so that the condemned man could command a view of his native land before the cart moved forward, leaving him suspended'. The sight also acted as a warning to other criminals. The *Three Ashes* was popular with the many gypsies who lived in that area. The licence was later taken over by the *Anne Boleyn* and houses were built on the site.

The wide and interesting variety of occupations in the town included wheelwrights, cordwainers and candlemakers. Mrs Letitia May of North Street made a living as a sausage maker, and George Thorogood is listed as groom and pew opener. By 1848, according to *White's Directory*, there were 1,722 people living in Rochford. Over half the inhabitants

68 North Street. The police station, on the left, is now the post office.

were agricultural labourers and around a quarter were shopkeepers. Benton says that shopkeepers in the whole of the hundred were renowned for giving short measure, were continually being fined for short weights, and were constantly being brought before the magistrates. The magistrates were little better. They were chosen for their wealth and position and not for their ability to administer the law and were often advised by the constables and thief catchers during hearings in the county court, which was held monthly at the *New Ship* inn. Petty sessions were held on alternate Thursdays at the *King's Head*, Mr William Swaine being clerk to both courts. In 1859 the County Court House, described in *White's Directory* as a handsome building, was erected in South Street at a cost of £3,000; it was built on the site of two old cottages. By today's standards some of the offences tried there are very trivial. Mr Horner was reprimanded for causing a nuisance by carting manure through the streets. Great Eastern Railway was found guilty of allowing manure to stand at the station. Charles Bibby was charged with causing an organ to be played; Inspec tor Chase had found him at Sparrow's together with 'a roundabout and steam organ and it was playing'. Bibby was fined 6s.11d.

There was no police force in the town until 1840 when the Essex County Constabulary was formed. There were 100 officers. Rochford was one of 14 divisions and had one superintendent, two constables at Rochford and two at Great Wakering. The headquarters was at Rayleigh. Officers had to pay 5s. when they received their uniform jacket. Helmets were made with reinforced frames strong enough for the officer to stand on in order to look over walls and fences. They were also useful for keeping sandwiches in, as the jacket had no pockets. It did, however, have a leather collar to protect the wearer against strangulation. The first superintendent at Rochford was 32-year-old Job Yardley, an ex-army man. His stay in Rochford was short-lived, and he absconded a few months after being appointed. The original police station was built in North Street in 1846. Prisoners were kept in two tiny cells in the basement. As the division increased in size, the building, which was intended for one superintendent and two officers, was soon found to be too small. The Corn Exchange had to be hired for four shillings a day to allow the superintendent to hold pay-parades and drills. By 1911 the Rochford division was made up of 28 parishes, whose population was nearly 94,000. There were 90 officers, 64 of whom were needed to police Southend. Southend then became a separate entity. Rochford and the small Dengie division became the new Rochford Division. By 1884 Rochford had one superintendent, one sergeant and 22 constables. The present Police Station in South Street was built in 1915 to accommodate one sergeant and three constables; it was opened in 1919. There were also two rented houses available for officers.

The fire service, like the police service, was disorganised and inept. Until 1666 the churchwarden was responsible for any fires that broke out in the parish. After the Great Fire of London, England's first fire brigades were formed and run by various insurance companies. The company would put a badge on the properties insured by them. One of these badges, belonging to Norwich Insurance Company, can be seen on a house in North Street. By 1865 the government had become involved and the Metropolitan Brigade was formed in London. Gradually more were organised and many other areas had their own volunteer fire fighters. The fire engines were merely a cart carrying a water tank pulled by two men; later, more sophisticated engines pulled by horses were introduced. The local fire engine was kept in a cottage in North Street now known as the Old Fire Station.

69 Superintendent Samuel Hawtree was in charge of the Rochford Division in 1886.

According to the *Southend Standard*, in 1908 fire broke out in the old tarred timbers of a barn at the Maltings, Weir Pond Road, at midnight one Sunday. The property belonged to

70 West Street, with Rochford Cycles and Willans the Grocer.

Mr Meeson of Battlesbridge. The fire brigade led by Mr Bacon attended with their hose cart and Southend Fire Brigade was summoned to help. Luckily the barn was empty apart from a few chickens. The authorities had not yet supplied the brigade with uniforms and, it being Sunday, the men were all wearing their best suits, which were ruined. A few weeks later another fire broke out, this time in Mr Morris' lock-up cycle shop. Fortunately a hydrant was nearby. The firemen entered the shop and put out the flames with the hand pump. Again they were wearing their own clothes. When fire broke out in the chemist's shop, two of the lads connected the hose to the hydrant outside the Women's Institute Hall and doused the flames. Harry Chapman, who was then Captain of the Rochford Brigade, was issued a summons by the Police Superintendent for stealing 3,000 gallons of water, property of the Rural District Council. Harry was taken to court where he explained that at the time of the fire he was at home with his slippers on! The Council were most displeased, but finally it was agreed that Harry was innocent and that in future there would be no charge for water used by the fire brigade to put out fires.

Eight

Education

There were several small private or dame schools in Rochford, for children of the well-to-do. The Ladies Academy, run by Miss Ann Allen, was later taken over by Mr George Foster, who came from Sydenham in Kent, and the school, situated in South Street, was called Sydenham House School. The school took boarders and day pupils. In 1864 a bill to the parent of one boy itemised: Board and education of son cost £5 a term, pianoforte 15s., pens 2s., copy books 6d. and drawing books 1s. 3d., small exercise 1s., pencil 1s. 3d., arithmetic 1s. 9d., note paper ½d, large exercise book 6d., slate pencils 2d., cutting hair 4d., ink 1s. 3d., blue cap 2s., belt 1s.

The first school in the town for children of the poor was the dissenter's school adjacent to the Congregational Chapel in North Street on land belonging to Samuel Tabor, to whom the Congregational church paid rent of £9 a year. The Congregationalists believed that education should be available to everyone. It is not certain exactly when the school opened but it was certainly before 1808, when the curate told the Archdeacon that there were three schools in Rochford, two of which were private and the other was attached to the dissenter's chapel. The first schoolmaster was Eli Beckwith, who was also a thatcher. He lived in the cottage which stood in the playground. The school had two classrooms, one down and one upstairs. Children from any religious persuasion were permitted to attend but had to pay a penny a week and supply their own pencils and slates.

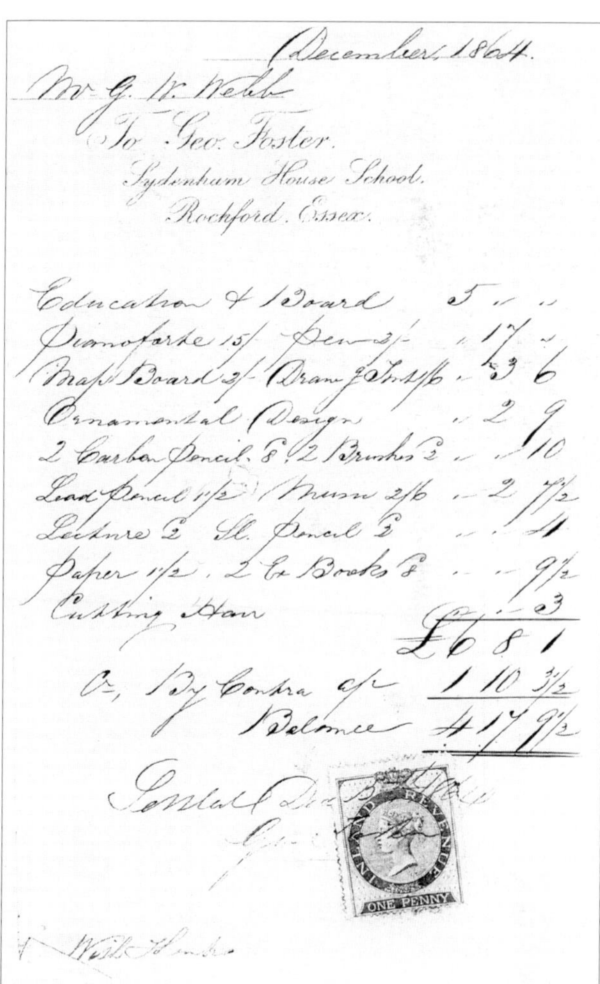

December 1864.

Mr G. W. Webb

To Geo. Foster.

Sydenham House School.

Rochford. Essex.

	£	s	d
Education & Board	5	..	..
Pianoforte 15/ Pens 2/	..	17	..
Map Board 2/ Drawg Bk 1/6	..	3	6
Ornamental Design	..	2	9
2 Carbon Pencil 8 / 2 Brushes 2	..	..	10
Lead Pencil 1/2 / Museum 2/6	..	2	7½
Lecture 2 Sl. Pencil 2	..	..	4
Paper 1/2 . 2 Cr Books 8	..	..	9½
Cutting Hair	..	..	3
	£6	8	1
Cr, By Contra a/c	1	10	3½
Balance	4	17	9½

Settled

71 Bill for Sydenham House School.

Later a third classroom was built for infants. Each year an anniversary service took place: children sang at services held in the church,

72 Drawing of Sydenham House School in South Street.

and played games on the meadow lent for the occasion by Mr Winterbon, a Rochford clothier; they were also treated to a tea and, later, fruit, nuts and cakes were distributed. A collection was taken for the school and Sunday School.

In 1837 a school board was set up and two schools were opened, one in Rochford and one in Great Wakering, managed by a joint committee. Later they separated, the Rochford School connected with the British and Foreign School Society and the one in Great Wakering with the Church of England. Every year the children came from Great Wakering in flower-decorated wagons to attend a service at Rochford Church and, afterwards, tea and games. The National School was held in St Andrew's Church Hall in West Street, and was run by Mr and Mrs Popplewell. There were two classrooms, one for girls and one for boys. Children travelled to the school from Eastwood, Sutton, Little Stambridge and Hawkwell. Pupils were expected to attend daily from Sunday to Friday. Saturday was a holiday. Children had to be over six years old and to have been vaccinated. The rules were strict: not being on time for school was a serious evil because late children would miss prayers; they set a bad example and would lose much valuable time. Pupils were given good marks for attendance, and when they received 12 good marks they earned one penny. At the end of the year the pennies were added up, and girls would be given dress material to that value and boys

73 Cottage in South Street opposite Sydenham House School.

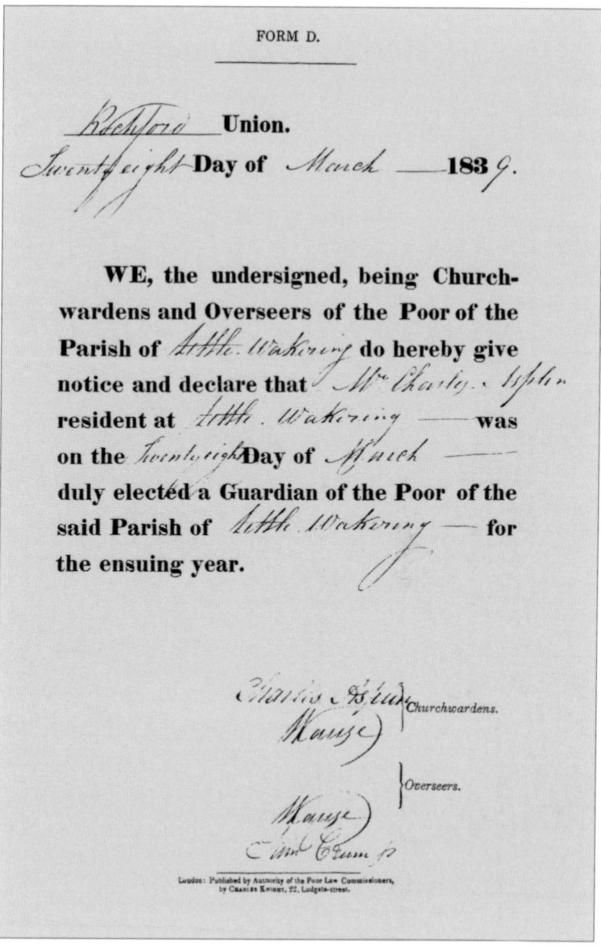

FORM D.

Rochford Union.

Twentyeight Day of March 1839.

WE, the undersigned, being Churchwardens and Overseers of the Poor of the Parish of Little Wakering **do hereby give notice and declare that** Mr Charles Asplin **resident at** Little Wakering **was on the** Twentyeight **Day of** March **duly elected a Guardian of the Poor of the said Parish of** Little Wakering **for the ensuing year.**

Charles Asplin, Mauze — *Churchwardens.*

Mauze, Wm Crump — *Overseers.*

London: Published by Authority of the Poor Law Commissioners, by Charles Knight, 22, Ludgate-street.

74 'Form D' declaring that Charles Asplin is elected Guardian of the Poor for Great Wakering.

would receive caps, socks and 'other useful articles'. By 1841 there were 218 children at the school.

THE UNION

While poor children were being given the chance of a better life so were the paupers, who were the responsibility of the parish. During the long war with France, relief for the poor had become a heavy burden on the local rates. People were going hungry, often having to suffer the indignity of being sent to the workhouse. Conditions were horrendous in many of these establishments. Following the reform of the Poor Law in 1834, zealous social reformer Edwin Chadwick arranged over 20,000 parishes into 600 unions, each with a workhouse and board of guardians supervised by commissioners at a central administration. The duties of the overseers were given to the guardians of the poor. The overseers became assessors and collectors. The first meeting of the Rochford Board of Guardians took place in the *King's Head*. The Board consisted of 27 people and the chairman was Thomas Brewitt JP from Rayleigh. Meetings were held every Thursday at 9a.m. Often there were only half a dozen members present. The landlady of the inn, Mrs Wilson, was paid five shillings for the use of one of her rooms.

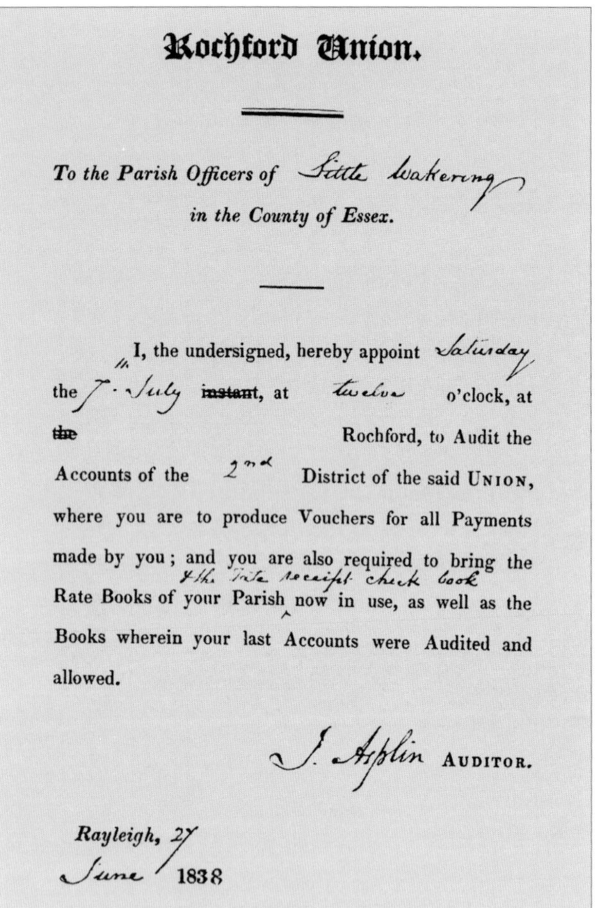

Rochford Union.

To the Parish Officers of Little Wakering
in the County of Essex.

I, the undersigned, hereby appoint Saturday the 7th July ~~instant~~, at twelve o'clock, at ~~the~~ Rochford, to Audit the Accounts of the 2nd District of the said UNION, where you are to produce Vouchers for all Payments made by you; and you are also required to bring the Rate Books of your Parish & the Rate receipt check book now in use, as well as the Books wherein your last Accounts were Audited and allowed.

J. Asplin AUDITOR.

Rayleigh, 27 June 1838

75 Rochford Union, or workhouse, was built to accommodate 300 inmates.

76 Rochford Union stone on the chapel.

The Rochford Union or workhouse was built in 1837 at the end of Union Lane, sometimes called Workhouse Lane. It was a fine building of yellow brick, able to hold 300 inmates. Despite the reforms, inmates suffered an appalling life. They lost their freedom, their dignity and their right to vote. They were subjected to strict and harsh treatment, poor food, squalid accommodation and a complete lack of privacy. They were made to do soul-destroying work such as rock breaking and oakum picking. Wives and husbands were parted, children were separated from their parents and brothers from sisters. The minute books of the Union tell of the brutal punishments meted out: one small boy was locked in a dark cupboard for two hours; a young girl who spoke to her brother was given a beating with a hairbrush. Christmas was the one time when the rules were relaxed: husbands and wives were allowed to meet and were given a feast of a roast dinner, plum pudding, sweets, and tobacco for the men, instead of the usual diet of bread and potatoes.

Between 1838 and 1851 there were 98 baptisms in the workhouse. Two of the mothers were widows, five were married, and the other 91 were single women. One desperate young girl put her newborn baby down the lavatory. Another unfortunate mother

77 The old chapel.

was Susan Gullock, spinster of Rochford, needlewoman and daughter of a clockmaker, who had two illegitimate children. The father of one, William Livermore, was forced to pay £2 16s. for the birth and sixpence a week maintenance. Rochford parish surgeon Dr John Grabham was paid £10 a year to look after any inmate who became ill. By 1859 the Board of Guardians ordered that paupers should be sent back to their own parish to be buried because the churchyard at Rochford was becoming overcrowded. Whenever possible children were found work with local families and were given bed and board in exchange for menial work. Labour was cheap. Most of the girls went into service; it was quite normal for all but the poorest families to have servants, or at least someone to do the 'heavy work'.

THE HOSPITAL

A new brick hospital was built in the grounds of the Union. It was officially opened in 1842 and could accommodate 50 chronically ill patients. The detached building, heated by open fires, was supposed to be visited by the medical officer once every day. It was soon found to be inadequate, outdated and far too small, so it was pulled down and replaced by a new one, which opened in 1858 and was insured for £1,000. There were four wards, a children's ward, a surgery and two small wards for infectious cases. Treatment was very primitive, the main drugs used being quinine, cod liver oil, castor oil and antimony. There was no piped water until 1863 and even then it was in short supply until eventual connection to the Southend waterworks. By the end of the century the Guardians decided to buy three

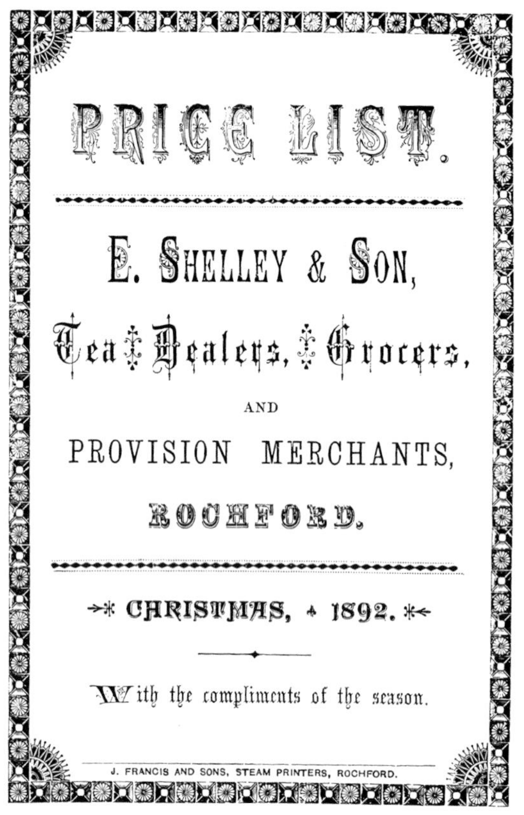
PRICE LIST.

E. SHELLEY & SON,

Tea Dealers, Grocers,

AND

PROVISION MERCHANTS,

ROCHFORD.

CHRISTMAS, 1892.

With the compliments of the season.

J. FRANCIS AND SONS, STEAM PRINTERS, ROCHFORD.

acres of land west of the workhouse and build a 30-bed ward for imbeciles and the feeble minded, a 24-bed ward for respectable and deserving infirm and 24 more beds for the less deserving. By 1903 a new set of rules for nurses was announced. Nurses on night duty were to be allowed out from 9a.m. until noon but had to be in bed by 12.30p.m. Day nurses were allowed out from 6p.m. to 9.30 one day a week if convenient. Lights out was at 10.30. By the 1920s this was called Rochford Hospital, and the wards were given names chosen from local parishes, such as Ashingdon, Canewdon and Chalkwell.

78 Shelley's shop was on the corner of the Square, where the Spar is now.

Nine

All Part of the Service

The delivery of letters was rather disorganised. In *A History of Rochford*, Cryer names George Poulton as Rochford's earliest postmaster, working from an inn, receiving £37 a year. He rode from Brentwood to Billericay, Wickford, Hockley and Rayleigh delivering the post. Later, Thomas White ran the post from his premises in Market Square. Letters arrived in Rochford at 4a.m. every morning and left at 6 p.m. every evening except on Sunday when they left at 5 p.m. The fee for delivery of letters varied from place to place. The 1841 census shows Henry Wood as postmaster, operating from the Hollies in West Street. *White's Directory* names him as postmaster in 1863 and mentions that money orders could be granted and paid at the post office and letters could be sent via Ingatestone. When Mr Wood retired after 26 years the appointment went to Mr Garood, who ran the office from his ironmonger's

79 The staff at the post office around the early 1920s.

80 Miss Burbridge receiving the Imperial Service Medal for 40 years' service in the Post Office.

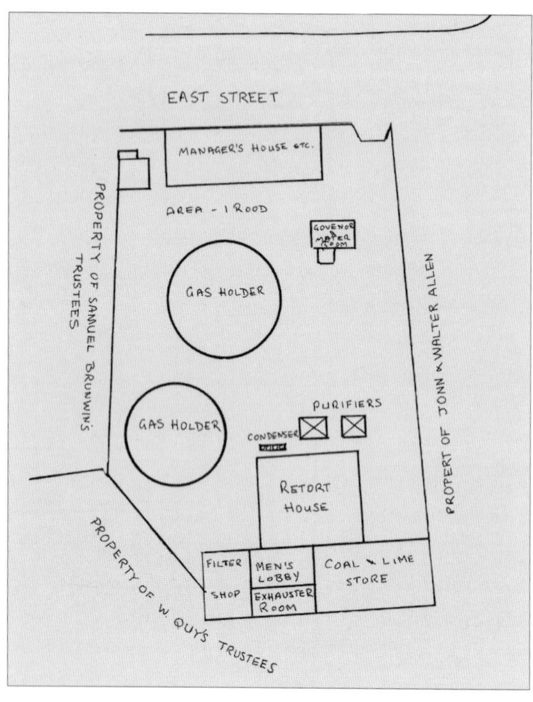

81 Plan of the gas works in East Street.

shop. Mail was dispatched from Rochford at 9 a.m. Letters posted five minutes before that time would arrive in London the same day. This was thought to be 'of great service to the tradesmen and others of the town and immediate neighbourhood'. Rowland Hill's scheme of 1840 to bring some unity to postal prices meant that for the first time postage stamps were sold in post offices, their price one penny. The first post office in Rochford was a room in a thatched house in North Street. Pillar boxes first made an appearance on the streets in 1852 but only in places where there were enough people to justify the expense. The present post office in North Street, originally the police station, was built in 1846. There were once two small cells in what is now the cellar.

The Rochford Gas Works was set up around 1845, and was privately owned. The last owners were a group of businessmen including Messrs

82 The Hall had become nearly derelict by 1867.

Asbey Taylor and Wood. After sixty years in private hands the company, situated in East Street, was taken over by Southend Gas Light and Coke Company in 1904 and remained in their hands for 16 years until it was closed down. It was finally dismantled in 1936. The old gas works site was where Grested Court is now.

The old Market Hall was finally replaced by the Corn Exchange (now the W.I. Hall), described by Pevsner as being modest in size and ugly in looks, built in 1866 on the site of the old inn called the *Vernon's Head*. It was built by a limited company with a capital of £1,250, and was governed by seven directors. F. Chancellor was the architect. Farmers would take their wheat samples there for verification but it also took over from the Market House as a meeting place for both farmers and locals. Numerous clubs and associations held their meetings in it. The Rochford Choral Society met there to entertain the elite of the area and in 1884 the Rochford Blue Ribbon Mission hired the building to bring the idea of teetotalism to Rochford. A choir of fifty voices and many famous orators made presentations on the evil of drink, drawing crowds each evening. The hall was packed every night, and many people took the pledge. The effects were not very far-reaching, however, for at Rochford Petty Sessions in 1888 there were 128 premises licensed to sell beer, refreshments and spirits in the town.

Next door to the Corn Exchange was the bank. The first known bank in the district was the Rochford Hundred and Billericay Bank. The partners were Matthew Barnard Harvey and John Whittle. This company failed and the business was taken over by W. and H. Mew, with no more success. Former manager James Giles, insurance agent, was next to run the bank, having been asked to do so by several

83 Grazing cattle were unpopular when the Golf Club took over the land around the Hall.

important men of the town, W.H. Rankin, T. Scratton and W. Kernot being three of them. Mr Giles began banking in 1830 and carried on until 1853. The business was taken over by Sparrow, Round, Green, Tuffnell and Round, who built the present bank in West Street in 1866. It was the only bank in the area and each week one of the staff was sent by special horse-drawn coach to the Marine Parade to conduct the banking business of Southend.

There were also important changes at this time at Rochford Hall. In 1867 the nearly derelict mansion and 408 acres of land were sold. The Hall was bought at auction for £25,000 by James Tabor JP, who then became the 42nd lord of the manor of Rochford. Mr Tabor bought several other lots including Brick Kiln Farm, Sutton Temple Farm and arable land abutting on 'Watery Lane, which is now called Ironwell Lane'. H. Mew purchased 23 acres of Rochford Hall fields near the rectory for £1,600. Property near Salt Bridge went to George Wood and Mr E. Boreham bought Workhouse Mead near the school for £1,240. Vendors wanting to preserve the avenue of trees in the road by the Hall stipulated that there would be a fine of £20 for each tree cut down. According to Tabor's nephew, the Hall was scarcely fit to live in and James wanted to stay at Earls Hall, where he had lived for some time although he was only a tenant there. He made a few rooms at the Hall habitable and persuaded his nephew George Savill to move in. In 1896 the east wing and some of the parkland was let to Rochford Golf Club. By November that year the club had 100 players and 40 ladies. A professional was employed to take charge of the grounds, the caddies and the coaching of members. His wage was 15s. a week. Players were disconcerted to find that sheep and cattle were still allowed to graze on the land and club rules had to be amended to allow any ball which landed in cow dung to be lifted, cleaned and dropped.

84 Some pupils from Rochford Boys School.

Education Acts sought to establish a national system of education for all children, and led to the development of schools looked after by local School Boards. One of the first in the country was built in Rochford. The Board consisted of W. Cowling, F. Francis, Miss Shelley and Rev. Barnard, who were appointed by Essex County Council, and Hugh Rankin JP and Arthur Stilwell by the Parish Council. William Gregson was Clerk to the Board and A. Cook of the Hollies was Attendance Officer. In 1877 the old National School was replaced by the Rochford Board School in Dale Road (now Ashingdon Road). Three separate schools were built to accommodate 400 children. One wing was for the boys and a corridor led to the girls' and infants' schools. Rochford Boys School opened first, then Rochford Girls School and, in 1896, the Infants School. Mr Culling, the head teacher, taught the older boys on a salary of £75 a year. Sometimes there would be 60 to 70 children in a class, and some of the children were described in the log book as 'big rough boys who caused disorder and disquiet in the class room'. One of these boys was repeatedly sent home for insubordination in which it seems he was encouraged by his parents. The log also tells of one boy being struck on the head by a pupil teacher and later dying from 'certain injuries'. A hearing found the teacher was not to blame.

Schooling was a rather haphazard affair for many of the local children. Those from farming families were needed at home to help at harvest time, with potato picking or pea picking, or in spring for scaring the birds. School was not free and children were expected to pay 6d. a week. Poor children were charged 2d., but even this was more than some families could afford so the children would sometimes be kept at home for weeks on end. Teachers were assessed on the children's attendance and results in examinations in the three Rs. The unfair system of 'payment by results' demoralised them

85 The staff of Rochford Primary School in 2002. Mr Rampersaud the headmaster is at the front centre.

and they sometimes resorted to sending the less able pupils to other schools for the day of the examination, and to passing the exam papers on to other schools.

The master in charge of the boys after Mr Culling was Mr Histed. He was headmaster for 38 years, retiring in 1927. The headmistress of the girls school was Miss Allen and the infants' headmistress was Miss Van Linschooten. In the playground was a stone bearing the date 1877. This stone is now inside, after the playground was used to build further classrooms accommodating 88 infants, when in 1896 the building was found to be too small. It was enlarged again in 1900, when more classrooms, a staff room and an office were added. Children of all ages were taught in the one school, although some lessons were taken in the church hall, but the Haddow Report of 1926 recommended that at 11 years of age children should be sent to new schools. When the new senior school was built in the Rocheway in 1937, Rochford boys, girls and infants were amalgamated, becoming Rochford Junior Mixed and Infants School. Some of the pupils were taught in the Wesleyan church school and the Legion Hall for another two years.

The School at Stambridge, called the Great and Little Stambridge Board School, also opened in 1877, under a Board of Guardians headed by the rector, the Rev. Penny. There were 48 pupils whose ages ranged from five to 13 years. By 1899 the roll had increased to 93 pupils. By 1966 there were 105 children on the roll and the name had been changed to The Great Stambridge Council School. There were still several small private schools at this time. Spotland House School, offering 'efficient education for girls and boys at moderate fees', was run by Mrs Howard, whose husband ran his builder's business from the same address. There was a small school in a house opposite the Hollies, and a little school in Brays Lane where the classroom was a disused railway carriage.

The school inspectors were shocked to find that Rochford School had only two outside toilets for 144 girls, but in the town houses were still being built without any sanitation at all. Water for washing and drinking had still to be fetched from the well and the pump in North Street had been condemned. The townspeople, angry that nothing was being done about the primitive and completely inadequate water supply, called a meeting of residents and ratepayers in the *King's Head* to discuss what should be done. Mr Harrington said he would be sorry to see the parish put to any expense and suggested that the Rural Sanitary Authority should be requested to rectify the matter. Mr Scott thought the supply was adequate: there were two wells in the town. The medical officer of health declared the pump water quite unfit and showed evidence of contamination.

86 (right) The Old Pump.

87 (below) The Great Eastern Station, where the notice board advertises a full summer service.

88 The Causeway, later renamed Station Road.

Rochford, Hockley and Rayleigh were finally supplied with piped water from Benfleet, which was later provided by Southend Waterworks Company. It was not until 1902 that the town pump was demolished. The town celebrated its passing with a procession through the streets, sports on Romney Marsh, special services in the church and a tea party for the children. Flags and illuminations decked the *Old Ship* and a bonfire was lit in Rutterford's meadow. A poem entitled 'The Poor Old Pump' was written in memoriam by Mr Francis the printer. The poem mentions the names of some of the tradesmen who looked after the pump and mourned its removal from the Square.

In 1883, when most people had never travelled further than the next village, and many could neither read nor write, the great whale which was captured by the crew of the fishing smack *Royal Albert* must have seemed one of the wonders of the world. The animal had been floundering in shallow water in the Crouch. It took five hours of laborious and hazardous work to slay the creature, which was towed into Creeksea where it was on view for three days. The huge animal was then taken to Southend on a trolley. People from miles around paid to see this strange creature which was over 30 feet long and 14 feet in diameter. It was put on show in Southend.

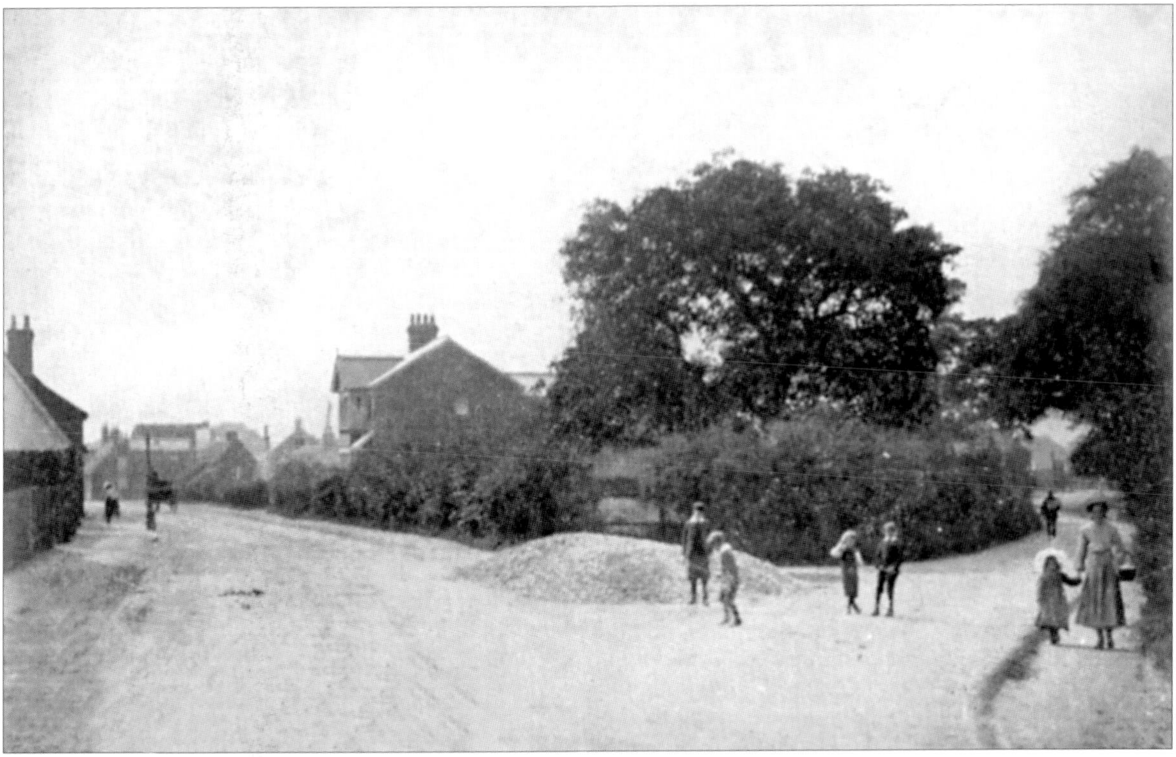

89 Weir Pond Road; the pile of stones would be spread across the road whenever it became too muddy.

ROCHFORD

Cricket Club.

DRAMATIC

ENTERTAINMENT

IN THE

Corn Exchange, Rochford,

WEDNESDAY, APRIL 29th, 1896.

Reserved Seats, 2/-. . . .

. . . . Unreserved Seats, 1/-.

Promenade, 6d.

Tickets to be obtained of Mr. WRIGHT, Chemist, (Successor to Mr. Harrington).

Doors open at 7-30. Commence at 8.

CARRIAGES AT 10 P.M.

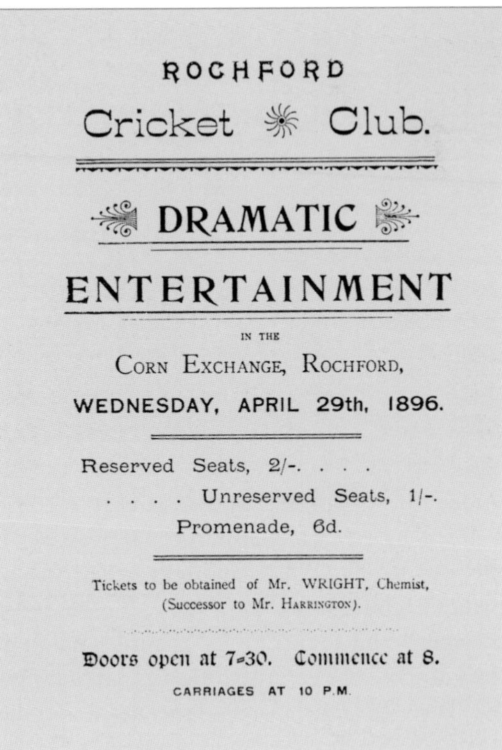

90 Rochford Cricket Club's entertainment.

The smack's owner, a Mr Page, assumed the fish was his but the lord of the manor of Burnham, Sir Henry Mildmay, claimed it was 'fish royal'. Eventually Mr Page gave up and the fish was deemed to belong to Henry Mildmay, who sold it to a professor so that the skeleton could be put into a museum in Sydney, Australia. The royalty of the river, 15 miles by one mile, had been granted to the Mildmay family by Edward III.

The majority of buildings in the town were built of wood and lit by candles or oil lamps so it was inevitable there would be frequent outbreaks of fire, although fortunately most were fairly small and easily extinguished –

unlike the great fire of 1884. This was first noticed by Mr Fulcher who was walking by the Board School late at night when he saw flames coming from the Square. He rushed to the scene and found fire and smoke billowing from the oil and colour workshop belonging to Mr Asbey. Mr Fulcher raised the alarm and then went to the *New Ship* and woke Mr Beeson, who went to call the fire brigade. Meanwhile about a hundred people had gathered in the Square. They pumped the well there dry, and those at the police station and the *New Ship*, in an effort to put out the fire but were unable to quench the flames, which spread to the property on either side and then to the *Star* beerhouse, which had stood in the corner

91 Horner's Corner from South Street.

of the Square for many years, and the stable and coach house at the police station. Eight cottages belonging to the Reverend Cotton were partly pulled down in an attempt to stop the fire. The fire brigade arrived from Southend. At three o'clock, three hours after it began, the fire was still raging, so the Army and their fire engine at Shoeburyness were sent for. They arrived bringing with them a large amount of hose which was taken to the brook where, luckily, there was plenty of water. By eight o'clock the next morning the fire was finally under control. Cottages in the alley were destroyed and eight families made homeless. Damage amounted to between two and three thousand pounds which was covered by insurance companies Norwich Union, The Phoenix, Essex, and Suffolk Royal.

Probably the most important change to the lives of ordinary people was the arrival of the railway. This had been in existence since 1840 but the line from London finished at Brentwood. Coaches brought passengers from there into Rochford and Southend. The LTS line from London to Southend had been in operation for some time and had proved so popular that the Great Eastern Railway, whose line ran from London to Colchester, planned a second route into Southend, joining the existing line at Shenfield. The single track railway finally arrived in Rochford on 1 October 1889. According to the *Southend Standard*, the first passenger train for Rochford, Rayleigh and London started at 7.15 a.m. from the 'spacious elegant Great Eastern Railway Station at Southend'. Mr Harrington of Rochford secured ticket no. 0001. On its arrival at Rochford there were no cheers, the crowd of about sixty people on the platforms seeming rather bemused and showing little enthusiasm. However, later in the day the town was decorated with banners and flags and crowds of people came to watch and cheer a procession of local traders as it left the Board School, drove through Church Street and on to Mrs Webster's Corner, then to Weir Pond Road and back to the station. The children were given a free trip to Wickford; adults had to pay one shilling a ride. So great was the demand that special tickets had to be made

Rochford Silver Jubilee Celebrations

MONDAY, MAY 6th, 1935.

Programme

OF THE

PUBLIC FESTIVITIES

IN COMMEMORATION OF THE

SILVER JUBILEE

OF

Their Most Gracious Majesties King George V. & Queen Mary

Whom God Preserve.

92 Silver Jubilee festivities, 1935.

on the station. Five hundred children were treated to a grand free tea in the goods shed. The proprietor of the *Kings Head*, Mr Taylor, provided a public luncheon at 2s. 6d. per head which was held in the Corn Exchange. In the evening the townspeople met in the County Court for a meal and entertainment.

There was no cause for celebration one morning in 1893 when the usually peaceful town was shattered at the news that a brutal murder had taken place. The *Southend Standard* records the murder that year of Mrs Emma Hunt and the arrest of labourer Alfred Hazell who had discovered the body. He explained that he had been returning from work that morning, and as he walked across the wilderness by the church he had seen the body of a woman lying face down by the pond. At first he thought she was asleep but when he looked more closely he found her throat cut, almost severing the head. Witnesses said they had seen Hazell running away from the area. He had blood on his hands and Superintendent Hawtree arrested him for

the murder but, despite thorough search of the area, no weapon was found. At the inquest, held at the *Old Ship*, the coroner decided suicide was unlikely and that Mrs Hunt from North Street had been murdered. Hazell was not convicted, and no one has ever been found guilty of her murder.

93 It was near the church that Mrs Hunt's body was discovered following her unsolved murder in 1893.

Ten

A New Century

The Relief of Mafeking in 1900 was the cause of great rejoicing throughout the whole country. The news reached Rochford at 2 p.m., and by the evening flags were flying and bunting adorned the shops and houses. The two brothers who ran the ironmonger's shop in the Square brought out their piano for a singsong. People from Rochford and the neighbouring villages gathered to celebrate the great victory and a huge bonfire was built in the Square. Locals threw anything they could lay their hands on into the blaze. Someone found an old farm cart in Stambridge Road, dragged it to the Square and heaved it onto the fire. Someone else went to the gas works for a barrel of tar which was thrown on. The wooden barrel soon burnt and the hot tar melted and ran down West Street, blocking the gutters and sticking to people's

94 The Avenue, later to become Hall Road. The wall on the left is part of the Hall.

shoes. The fire was becoming dangerously out of control so people tried to extinguish it by throwing on sand and earth and, finally, water. Eventually it was quelled and the party ended.

Just months later, in January 1901, the world was saddened at the death of Queen Victoria. The following year Edward VII's coronation took place. The local newspaper tells of a continuous stream of flags from the *Horse and Groom* right through the town. A service taken by the Rev. Cotton was held in St Andrew's Church, after which people gathered in the Square. The Burnham town band could be heard wherever you were. Decorated bicycles and vehicles paraded through the streets, and were judged by the Rev. Cotton. Mr F. Francis mounted a lorry in the midst of the people to record the Royal Address wishing the King well after his illness and asking God's blessing on him and her gracious Majesty Queen Alexandra, and wishing them a long and happy reign. The National Anthem was sung and the celebrations began with a procession through the streets and 'athletic sports' played on Romney Marsh, followed by tea for the under-15s and over-60s and a bonfire. Mugs bearing the 'usual royal device' on one side and a 'capital representation of the Town Pump' on the other were presented to the committee by Dr Young. Cards with gold printing on blue and white made pleasing mementoes for the prizewinners.

In 1911 the coronation of George V took place, with services in the parish church and in the Wesleyan Chapel. Residents gathered in the Square, where Mr Tabor led them in singing the National Anthem. In the afternoon the schoolchildren marched to Romney Marsh for athletic sports and a bicycle gymkhana. Tea was provided for 600 children and all were presented with a coronation mug. The best decorated and lighted house competition was so popular that it had to be divided into two sections, one for houses with a rateable value of over £12, and one for those under £12. The evening ended with a splendid firework display.

At the beginning of the new century motorcars began to make an appearance on the roads, the first flight in a heavier-than-air machine took place, old-age pensions were started and the women's suffrage movement began. However, it was not long before Rochford, with the rest of the world, prepared for 'the War to end all Wars'. An advertisement in the local paper read, 'Your Country needs you. Every day is fraught with the gravest possibilities, at this very moment the Empire is on the brink of the greatest war in the history of the world. All unmarried men join the army today.' Civilians were given instructions explaining what to do if the Germans marched into Rochford. Plans were drawn up and escape routes arranged. Men were told to take their tools and be prepared to work. Owners of horses and farm animals would have to hand them over or destroy them. Families should take their money, food and blankets to collecting points. Tents were pitched on the grass by the Hall and army mules were kept by Keeper's Cottage. Whenever they heard the sirens the families from nearby cottages would gather for shelter alongside the long high wall outside the Hall. The Golf Club was ordered to plough up the golf course for the cultivation of vegetables.

During the war a large aerodrome was built just south of Rochford which was completely self-sufficient, even having its own power supply. There were 11 fatalities there during the conflict. The War Office listed Rochford Airport as one of the potential sites for a Royal Flying Corps Home Defence Aerodrome, as it was thought to be an important link in the Essex chain around London. By 1916 Rochford was a night landing ground. The first sortie ended with the Bleriot aircraft making a forced landing on Leigh Marshes. The next was in

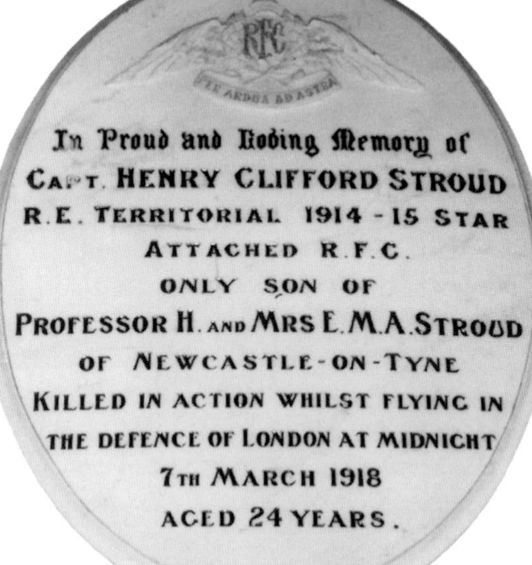

95-6 Propeller memorial to Captain Stroud, whose aircraft crashed in 1918, and Captain Stroud's memorial in Rochford church.

1916 in pursuit of a Zeppelin; this time our aircraft was forced to land in Thameshaven. Rochford Aerodrome was described as a magnificent aerodrome almost a mile square. Various squadrons operated from here, one of which was 61 Squadron. In March 1918 Captain Stroud of 61 Squadron collided with Captain Kynoch. Their aircraft were returning home after attacking the enemy on one of the last raids over London. The accident took place by the railway line, halfway between Rayleigh and Wickford and two memorials mark the spot where they crashed. Captain Stroud is buried in Rochford church and there is a memorial to him there; Captain Kynoch was buried in Golders Green. The land upon which they crashed was sold some time later but the piece of ground containing the memorials was not included in the sale and is to be held forever sacred.

A Gotha, a three-seater biplane bomber, was hit by anti-aircraft fire from a battery on Canvey Island. The pilot tried to land at Rochford Aerodrome but crashed into a tree on the golf course. His cargo of two aerial torpedoes, a gas bomb and 68 incendiary bombs was removed but unfortunately the machine was accidentally set on fire and destroyed. The commander and two officers were taken prisoner. Prisoners-of-war were kept in a block in the old workhouse. They worked on the farms, ploughing, bringing in the harvest, repairing hedges and ditches and doing numerous other jobs on the farms. Another ward at the workhouse, the aged and infirm block, was turned into a military hospital. A memorial on the north wall of the parish church names the men of Rochford who died in the Great War. Poppy wreaths are placed there every Armistice Day.

97 People gathered in the Square to celebrate the ending of the First World War.

After the war was over, 61 Squadron stayed in Rochford until 1919. It was then that civil aviation and pleasure flying began at the aerodrome. Southend Flying Club started in a field in Ashingdon. Their preferred aircraft was a tiny machine named the Flying Flea. These were available in kit form and many members built their own. The greatest Flying Flea rally of all time was held there. Enthusiasts brought their aircraft from as far away as France, some by road, some flying. At least one crashed into a tree, one caught fire, an auto-giro overturned and others failed to get off the ground, much to the amusement of the crowd. The Flying Club's stay in Ashingdon was short, and they soon moved to an airstrip in the centre of Rochford Pony Track, where the Flying Circus was a frequent visitor; pilots would perform all kinds of daring tricks and aerobatics, bursting balloons with their wing tips. Hundreds of people came to witness the spectacle, including parties of schoolchildren. In 1935 the club transferred to the new Southend Municipal Airport by Warner's Bridge. The racecourse was between Dalys Road and Brays Lane, the grandstand backing onto Ashingdon Road. Rochford Coursing Club held many successful meetings there, with up to thirty dogs taking part. Pony racing also attracted hundreds of visitors to

98 Tablet in St Andrew's Church in memory of the men of the parish killed in the Great War.

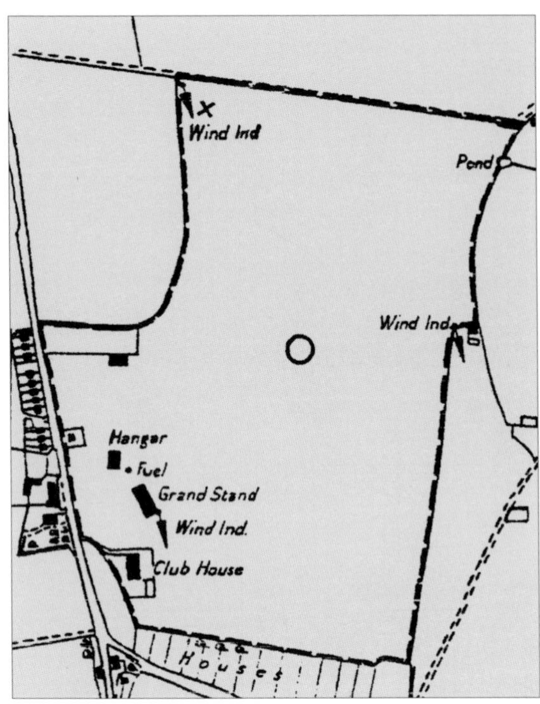

99 Map of the old Rochford Aerodrome.

the area, the railway running special trains for the occasion.

At the beginning of the First World War, the Corn Exchange fell into disuse and was sold to Miss Tawke of Bullwood Hall. Miss Tawke was very beautiful and a great character, a writer and a fine horsewoman who never tired of working for the good of the less fortunate people of the area. She turned the Corn Exchange into a laundry in order to provide work for some of the 'unfortunate women' she had taken under her wing. At the end of the war she let the building to two demobbed men who opened the Corn Exchange Garage; Francis and Baker, motor and cycle engineers, were there until 1922. That same year the Women's Institute was formed, their first meeting taking place at Swaines. Later they moved to the school but soon tired of having to carry in the coal to make up the fire, so changed venue to the Court House, which they rented for £7 a year. They managed to buy a piano, but this proved to be a mixed blessing, for the neighbours complained about the noise. The ladies decided it was time to buy a permanent meeting place and Miss Tawke sold them the Corn Exchange for £800.

About this time the Bentall family were preparing to leave Rochford Hall and the Hurst family were looking forward to moving in. Cecil Arthur Hurst, his wife Gertrude and two-year-old son Oswald took over the 600 acres that included the present airport and golf club. Also included were mooring rights

ROCHFORD PARK RACES,
AUGUST 24, 1898.

YOU ARE INVITED TO PARTAKE OF
LUNCHEON IN THE
STEWARD'S ENCLOSURE.
WITH COMPLIMENTS FROM
J. WALKER,
CHAIRMAN.
LUNCHEON WILL BE LAID from 12 till 2 p.m.

100 Invitation to the Steward's Enclosure, 1898.

101 Charabanc trip leaving from the *New Ship*.

at Fleet Hall on the Crouch. Hay and straw were sent from here to London and manure was brought back. The 200 cows, calves, ewes and lambs were tended by men living in the farm cottages and the shepherd who lived in the present Shepherd's Cottage. There was no piped water at the Hall, but several wells, one conveniently under the enormous kitchen, and a pump near the staircase. There was no electricity either, cooking being done over an open fire or by oil stove. There was a bathroom upstairs but water had to be carried up in large jugs. The toilet was outside. Mains water was eventually supplied in 1946 and electricity a

year later. The Hursts and their sons Oswald, Frances and Elwyn were the last farm tenants to live at the Hall. The Golf Club purchased the part of the Hall they had formerly rented, and the barns were used as storage and pigsties. These were later restored and became five large luxury houses.

By 1939 the country was at war again. Anthony Eden, Secretary of State for War, appealed on the radio to men between 17 and 65 to enrol as Local Defence Volunteers. There was a great response locally. The Paglesham and Stambridge group met at the Trout Fisheries tearoom. The Ashingdon contingent met in Ashingdon Road, and the Rochford branch held their meetings in a house opposite the fire station. Churchill called them the 'Home Guard' and the name stuck. Their duties included checking on any strangers in the

102 Mr Samuel Joseph Hill. The Hill family ran the photographer's shop in East Street.

103 New homes were built at the back of the Hall.

104 Sutton Barling and Wakering Platoon, D Coy.

105 The Ashingdon Platoon outside Ashingdon Hall.

106 Rochford Home Guard.

area, making sure the blackout regulations were kept and keeping a lookout for any enemy activity, but they also guarded the ration books that were kept in a house next to the fire station. A man sat on guard with a rifle and five bullets from 8 p.m. to 6 a.m. He was paid 2s. 6d. At 6 a.m. he handed in the keys to the police station.

Sandbags were stacked against the shops and lawns were dug up to grow vegetables in the 'Dig for Victory' campaign. All through the war, Rochford market stayed open since it was one of the most important stock markets in the area. The cattle were brought in by train and kept in pens near the Freight House, then driven along a cinder path in West Street to pens on the corner of the Square near the present library, where they were tied by their horns to the railings. They frequently escaped and local lads would give chase. Bollards were erected in Market Alley to stop the animals dashing down North Street. Sheep and pigs were usually brought by road, pig and sheep hurdles being kept in the yard of the *King's Head*. Chickens, ducks and rabbits were also sold from the *King's Head* yard.

At the railway station sugar beet, corn and potatoes were loaded from a siding near the Freight House. On the platform would be wicker baskets holding carrier pigeons, the birds being set free by the porter at the precise time of the race start. Air-raid shelters were built: Andersons, made of corrugated metal, were put up in gardens; Morrisons, low, metal, cage-like constructions were erected indoors; and concrete shelters were built outside schools and offices. Evacuated children from Chingford and Rainham were housed in the school until homes could be found for them. The school then taught the evacuees in the mornings and local children in the afternoons. A year later all the evacuees and 136 local children left Rochford. The children and their teachers met at the station at 6a.m. on 2 June. Each child carried a gas mask, sandwiches and a drink. No one knew where they were going until they arrived in Bream, a small mining village in the Forest of Dean, Gloucestershire. The school

107 The war memorial at the corner of Weir Pond Road; there is a move afoot to resite it to a more convenient place.

WORLD WAR 1939—1945.

SOUVENIR PROGRAMME

OF

-:- VICTORY -:-

CELEBRATIONS

ROCHFORD

Saturday, 8th June, 1946,

Organised by Rochford Peace Memorial Committee.

President : ALEC STEEL, ESQ.

Price Sixpence.

108 Souvenir programme of Victory Celebrations, 1946.

was reopened later that year for the children whose parents had refused to let them go or who had returned home from Bream. Lessons were often taken in the air-raid shelter built on the field across the road.

All patients at the hospital were evacuated to the ground floor. Blast walls were built, volunteers filling thousands of sand bags. Appeals were made for fresh fruit, vegetables and eggs. There was a serious water shortage, so huge concrete storage tanks were constructed. After the war they were converted into fishponds. In 1941 Johnson Ward was bombed, but fortunately there were no casualties. Bombs landed in Dalys Road and Somerset Avenue and there was considerable damage to the Methodist Chapel in North Street. The nurses' home was taken over by the fire brigade and air-raid wardens patrolled at night. Because of the shortage of men, women were employed for the first time as hospital porters. German aircrew shot down in local fields were brought to the hospital, some of the nurses learning German so they could communicate with them. Some went as volunteers to funerals when there was no one to mourn a young German airman. In 1940 a 100lb. bomb destined for RAF Rochford fell in the farmyard at the Hall. Nineteen bombs landed on the golf course, fortunately doing little damage.

The W.I. Hall was in great demand for First Aid courses and money-raising events.

The territorial recruiting campaign was held there, the ladies providing tea for the 70 men who attended. The 6th Battalion of the Essex Regiment was there for two hours a week and the ARP rented it for a year. They used the basement to store blankets, palliasses, feeding bottles, chamber pots, galvanised baths, and anything that might be needed by the children brought in to the reception centre, including hundreds of children from London. The W.I. bought a canning machine. People could take their fruit along and have it canned for a few pence. A thousand pounds of fruit was canned under the guidance of the Ministry of Food. Any sub-standard produce was sent to the British Restaurant in South Street. British Restaurants were set up all over the country, providing good hot meals at reasonable prices, for which coupons were not needed. Rochford's opened in 1942, and comments in the visitors' book suggest it was one of the best and provided an excellent lunch. Food parcels were sent to the W.I. from Australia and New Zealand. These were a godsend, food and soap being shared out among the members, and cigarettes and woollen clothes sent to relatives who were serving in the forces. The W.I. welcomed home the troops with a grand party in the Hall.

V.E. Day was celebrated in style with flags, bunting and street parties. At the hospital the end of the war was celebrated with double pay for everyone and the removal of the blast walls. A small memorial was erected at the corner of Weir Pond Road and East Street naming some of the men who were killed in action.

Eleven

Post-War Days

The great floods of 1953 devastated much of the area around the Essex coast, causing many deaths and hundreds of ruined homes. Canvey Island was completely submerged, 58 islanders losing their lives. The river burst its banks at Paglesham and Foulness but Rochford remained relatively dry. A row of houses in Ashingdon was donated by the Norwegians to mark their sympathy for the disaster.

Later that year the whole country rejoiced at the coronation of Queen Elizabeth II. Elaborate celebrations took place in Rochford. A united service was held in the Square, followed by fancy dress parades, a fête, comic football matches, open-air dancing, a pony gymkhana and children's parties. The W.I. Hall was open for anyone to watch the event on television. The new Elizabethan era saw the beginning of changes in the town. There was still much

109 West Street. The notice board on the left advertising the *Southend Pictorial* predicts 'more flooding than usual this winter'.

110 Flood Houses. Twenty houses were given by the people of Norway after the flood disaster of 1953.

poverty and a housing shortage, with 750 applicants waiting for homes, so the council made plans for the building of the Rochford Garden Estate.

Some of the old businesses in Rochford had been forced to close down, but new ones began to emerge. At one time there was a large brewery behind the *Cherry Tree*. An inventory of 1834 shows it had belonged to Henry Lambirth since 1803. There was a horse wheel 15 feet in diameter and a well 60 feet deep. The inventory valued the property at £5,623 7s. In 1836 Lambirth moved to Chelmsford and sold the business to John English. By 1874 Stambridge Brewery was listed as being in joint ownership with the Middleton Brewery of Henry Luker and Co. of Southend; the *Cherry Tree* was the brewery tap house. The wide selection of beers included Old Beer, Old Mild, Mild and Table Beer. The main part of the brewery was demolished in the 1930s. Behind the *Cherry Tree* is Winters, once the home of the owner of the old brewery.

Mrs Mead and family lived in a four-roomed one-storey house belonging to the brewery. One very high tide caused extensive flooding in the area and left their house almost submerged, just the roof showing above the water. Amid the chaos Mrs Mead gave birth to a baby boy and named him Noah; the cottage became known as Noah's Ark. The cottage had originally been a three-sided brick shed but the owners added a wall and turned it into a house.

Wall's Creamery was started in 1903 by John Wall. John came to Magnolia Road from Ilkley

111 The weekly cattle market was held in the Square.

112 Greetings from Rochford.

113 Cottages in Ship Lane, with King's Hill in the background.

in Yorkshire. He had a small herd of dairy cows and sold milk from his horse-drawn van. After ten years he started the Ashingdon Dairy Farm and opened a small shop near the *Victory* in Ashingdon Road. Beside the shop was a small thatched house built by German prisoners kept in the hospital. Wall's next move was to North Street. In 1927 John's son, Henry, opened a shop in Weir Pond Road, and by 1932 the family had bought Fir Tree Dairy Farm in East Street from Rankin. Their herd was of 13 cows but they collected milk from other nearby farms and cream from Eccles Dairy in Southend. They delivered milk twice a day until the war, first by horse and cart and later by Model-T Ford with wooden wheels. By 1951 pasteurisation had arrived and Walls' bought in bottled milk from the wholesaler. The business passed from generation to generation ending with Adrian, who ran the dairy from Riverside Industrial Estate behind the fire station. This closed in March 2002 when it was taken over by Dairy Crest.

Whittingham's Garage is the oldest company still in business in the town, and one of the ten oldest in the county; it was started by Joseph Whittingham, who was born in 1807 at the Gore, Stambridge and opened the business in 1830. It manufactured coaches and agricultural machinery. Joseph also opened a brass and iron foundry employing four blacksmiths and two woodworkers. The business, in Union

114 Whittingham's Garage opened in 1830.

Lane, was carried on by his five sons. The first carriages they made had wooden wheels bound with iron. A two-wheeled cart cost £80; four-wheeled wagons retailed at £120. Joseph's grandson, William Hale Wittingham, started repairing motorcycles in the wagon works. Two blacksmiths worked for the company, Hubert Bacon opposite the *Rose and Crown*, and Jack Topsfield on the corner of Union Lane. Whittingham's obtained their first licence to store fuel in 1906. The present garage and petrol station, built in 1924, is run by Joseph's great-grandchildren.

Cottis and Sons opened in 1829. When the railway arrived Mr Cottis realised the potential for a haulage business carrying parcels to and from the station. From one cart and two horses the company grew into the biggest haulage

115 One of the early Model T Fords built by Whittingham's.

company in the area. By 1981 the company ran 30 vehicles. Rochford-born Norman Cottis started working for the firm when he left school in 1934. Six generations have run the business, which was taken over by British Road Services in 1949, but the family bought part of it back three years later. Norman expanded the business and went into the building trade, purchasing a site on the Sutton Road Industrial Estate in the 1960s. Its speciality was bricks.

One of the new companies to open a branch in Rochford was run by Eric Kirkham Cole. Soon after broadcasting began in the 1920s, he opened a small shop in Westcliff selling wireless batteries and charging accumulators. One of his customers, William Verrells, offered to invest £50 in the business. They went into partnership, left the shop and set up in larger premises over a shop in Westcliff. By 1930 Eric had bought a huge piece of land at Prittlewell, where he built a factory and sold wireless sets, at first made of sheet metal and later of bakelite. He also operated in part of the old Gliderdrome in Southend. The next step was to produce televisions, originally black and white but later colour. Ekco soon

116 Topsfield, the blacksmith's, on the corner of Union Lane.

117 Church Street; Whittingham's is on the far right.

118 Looking along Church Street, now West Street, towards the Square.

119 The cattle market in the Square.

became one of the largest employers in the area. Their radar equipment was invaluable during the war. By 1961 Cole had a factory in Rochford, the Ekco Electronics Works on the Sweynes Industrial Estate off Ashingdon Road, but this closed down around 1969 causing much unemployment in the area.

The old Ekco building was taken over by Lesney's toy factory. In the first year production trebled. At one time over 2,000 people were employed there working both day and night shifts, making model cars. Special Lesney buses brought workers in from Shoebury, Southend and Rayleigh. The company wanted to build a road around the estate, but locals complained about the number of huge lorries that would be thundering past their houses. It wasn't long before the firm ran into difficulties: many people lost their jobs and shares were suspended. The company continued trading under a different name, Matchbox, and its fortunes fluctuated. New toy fairs brought hope and big orders for the new 'Superfast' cars poured in but staff were taken on only to be made redundant shortly afterwards. After many troubled years the factory finally closed, Matchbox eventually moving to China. The land was taken over for a huge housing development.

HOOVER
J.M. YOUNG
ALTERATIONS
Rochford Coach

120 Rochford Carnival entry, 1962: Sid Dowell and Ringo.

121 The Beach was a popular spot for a day out.

One interesting business that grew up in Rochford was the Tag Company. They manufactured a tiny electronic radio transmitter, which was fixed to a plastic tag and attached to goods in shops. The assistant would remove the tag when the goods were paid for. If the item were taken out of the shop before the device was removed, an alarm would sound. These proved a great success. The business grew in just over a year from a cottage industry to one with a multi-million-pounds turnover, employing a hundred staff. The factory opened from 8a.m. to 10p.m. each day. UK agents employed Ronnie Barker, in his TV role as 'Fletcher' from *Porridge*, to advertise the benefits of the tag.

With the closure of Ekco and Matchbox, work became scarce in the town and people were forced to commute, mainly to London or Southend.

Twelve

Time of Change

The 1960s was a period of great changes in Southend. Big old Victorian houses were demolished to make way for high-rise flats and office blocks, including a huge Civic Centre. Fashionable shops, supermarkets and restaurants wooed shoppers away from the smaller towns. Rochford was left behind, its quaint old buildings and narrow streets remaining virtually the way they had been for years. In 1901, away from the four main roads, Ashingdon Road had just seven houses and the fever hospital, and there were a few houses in Church Street and a few cottages in Barrack Lane, Weir Pond Road and Stambridge Road. By 1940 a score of new roads had appeared and the population had increased to around 4,000. The council had plans to make major changes, intending to modernise the whole town and

122 The junction of the four roads. Selby's is on the corner of South Street.

123 The corner of North Street; the shop on the right is the tobacconist and lending library.

turn it into a thriving commercial centre: some of the unmade roads were at last made up and the ancient houses in South Street were scheduled for demolition and replacement with modern flats and offices. But the scheme was immediately turned down by Essex Council planners, because the cottages made positive architectural and historical contributions to Rochford. The rural district council bought Roche House in South Street for £5,750 because of its great architectural interest. Buildings on the north side of the Square were to be pulled down and replaced with modern shops and the Square made into a pedestrian precinct. A new road parallel with West Street and a new bypass to the east of the town would take the lorries to the timber wharves, the mill and the gravel pits at Creeksea. After two years most of this project was abandoned.

The amount of heavy traffic through the narrow streets had greatly increased over the years and from 1958 Rochford residents were asking for a bypass. The advent of the promised road was delayed by the government because of lack of money. However, finally, in 1962, the Ministry of Transport conceded that the road was being considered; plans were in hand to start work in two years' time. The council agreed to spend £125,000 on a bypass which would begin at South Street near Salt Bridge and end in Hall Road. Once the scheme was underway it would be necessary to divert the Roach and re-site the reservoir. Nearly 450 trout, tench, bream, carp and roach were taken out of the pond, stored at the Stambridge Fisheries, and brought back when the work was completed. The bypass, named Bradley Way after the County Surveyor, was opened in 1967.

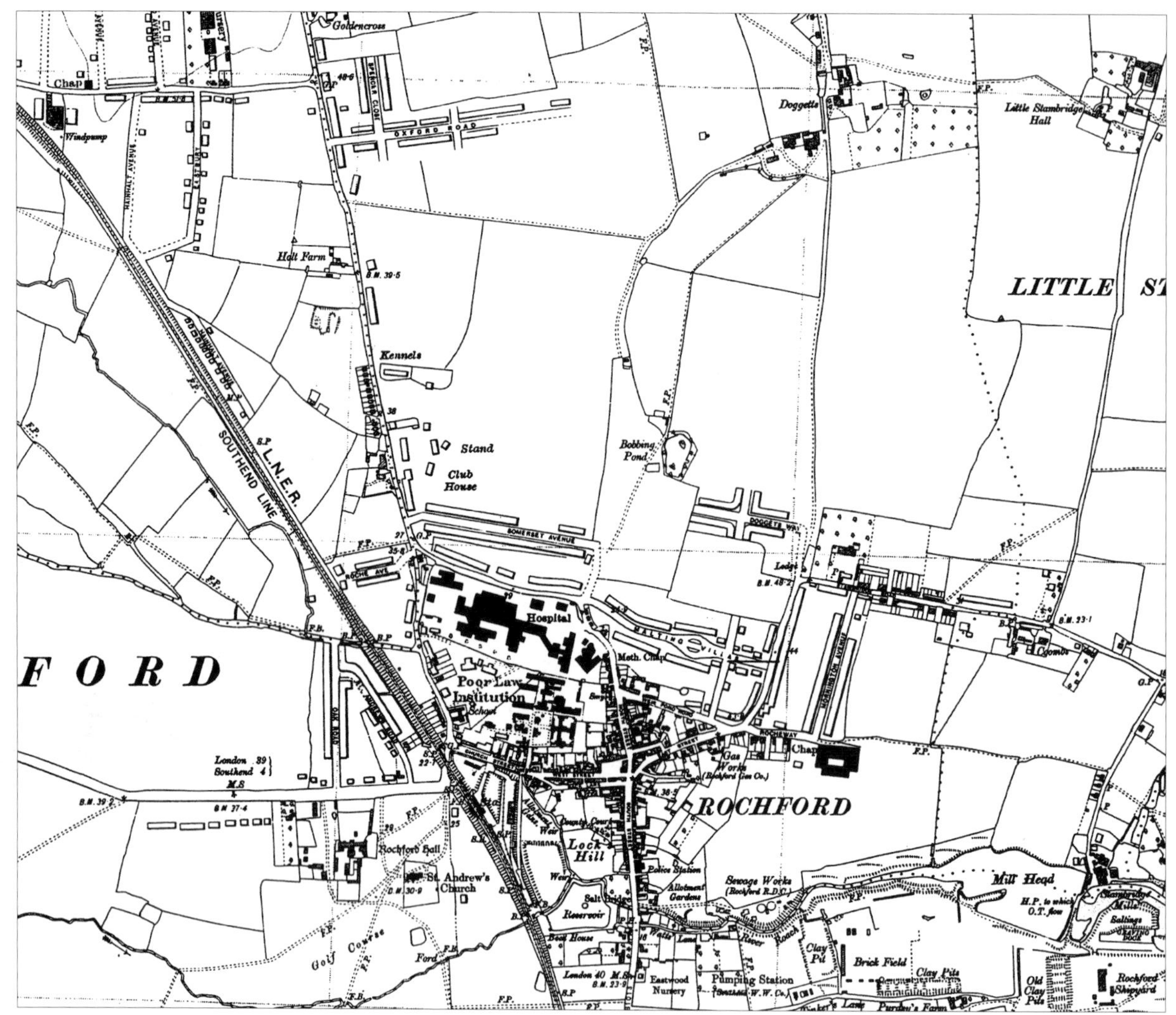

124 A map of 1938 showing the housing in the town.

In 1967 a meeting was held to discuss forming a Rochford Historical Society. So many people attended that some had to stand outside and listen from the window. It was intended to be part of the Amenities Society, but the interest was so great it was decided it should stand in its own right, with Sir John Ruggles Brise, Lord Lieutenant of the County, as its president. There were over 200 members in the first year. The society was devoted partly to saving the ancient buildings in the district and one of its first battles was the fight to save the 16th-century house known as King's Hill.

In 1969 Rochford Council bought King's Hill for £26,000 with a government loan. Because of its historical value a preservation order was placed on it and on the cottage which stood in its grounds. Both were included in the local government's list of buildings of special architectural or historical interest. The council then withdrew the order, now saying the building was of no architectural value which boasted nothing to warrant its retention, so

125 The newsagent's shop on the south side of the Square being pulled down. The tanning salon is here now.

it was to be pulled down and a block of flats erected in its place. The County Council turned down the offer to turn it into a library or museum, saying it was unsuitable. Locals were furious at the proposal to demolish the ancient property and petitions were organised, many members of the public writing letters of objection. Arguments between the council and the preservationists lasted over 18 months, Rochford Historical Society and local MP Sir Bernard Braine joining in the battle to preserve the historic house. King's was left empty and boarded up until in 1972 it was finally saved and sold to a private Southend buyer. The ancient Whispering Post still stands in the grounds and the deeds stipulate that it must never be removed.

During the late 1960s the almshouses were deemed to be unfit. They escaped demolition thanks to the persistence of Councillor Vic Bland who, finally, with help from the Charity Commission persuaded Rochford Rural District Council to agree to an interest-free loan to upgrade the buildings and modernise

126 The Square in the 1960s. There was a bus stop on the left before the one-way system was introduced.

127 A map dated 1960 shows the extent of new building in the town.

the interiors. During the year it took to complete the renovations, the residents were housed in the old nurses' home in South Street. The almshouses had damp courses and central heating installed, and the kitchens and bathrooms which had been added in the 1930s were modernised.

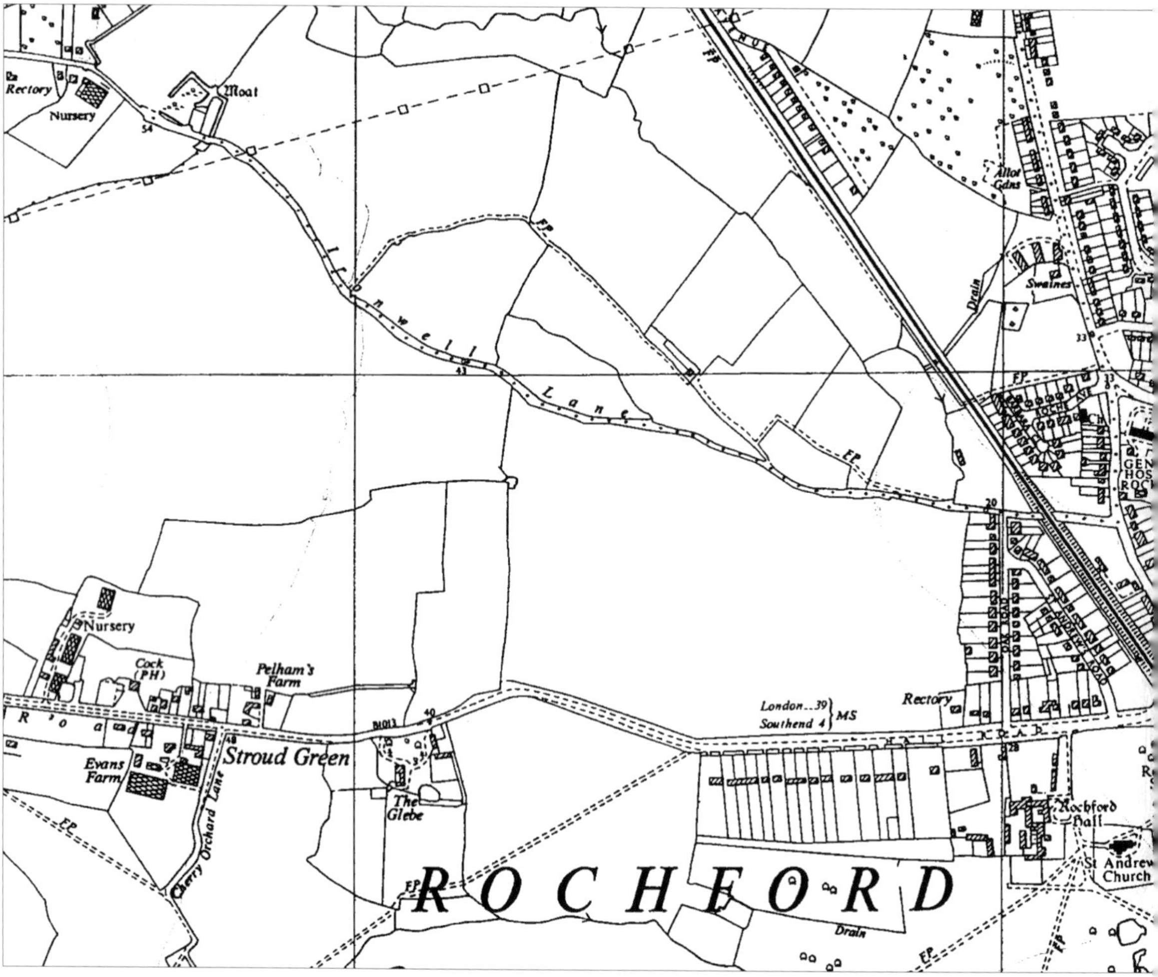

The 1960s was the heyday of Southend Airport. Aircraft left all through the day and night for the Channel Islands and the continent. Channel Airways, run by Jack Jones, operated Bristol freighters converted to carry cars, Vikings, Dakotas and the Golden Viscounts. BUAF (British United Air Ferries) flew DC-4s converted to car-carrying Carvairs. The package holiday was at its height and nearly a million passengers a year used the airport. But as aircraft got bigger and heavier the runways became inadequate. The main runway would have to be extended, which would mean demolishing some of the old cottages in Eastwoodbury Lane, and there was strong public opposition to the proposal. The matter was finally resolved when the government decided against the extension. The airport was still used by smaller aircraft, for maintenance and freight, but the large companies relocated, causing hundreds of people to lose their jobs. Part of Channel Airways moved to Stansted but the company went into liquidation in 1972.

Rochford Secondary Modern School, built in Rochway in 1937, was closed owing to its proximity to the airport. The noise from aircraft was disturbing and the school was considered to be in a danger zone. A new school, King Edmund's, was built in Vaughan Close; the old school is now the Adult Community College. The loss of jobs at the airport was another blow to the economy of Rochford. Property became empty and shops closed as people decided to move or commute. The council revealed new plans to take Rochford into the next century. Councillor Stan Robinson was quoted in the *Southend Standard* as saying that nothing in the town was worth saving. The same paper also

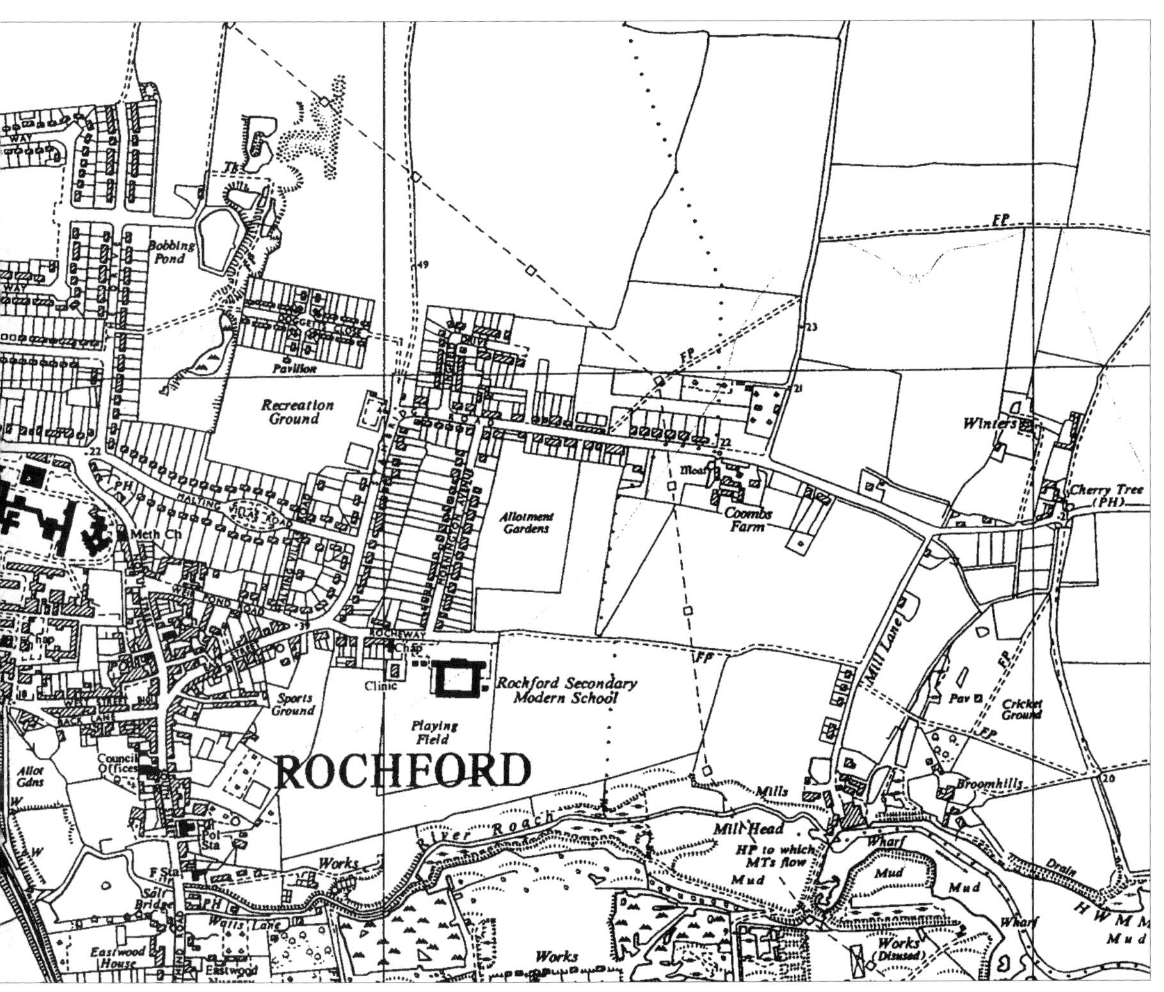

128 Emma Hunt's cottage in North Street, between the Congregational Church and the *Old Ship*. Mrs Hunt was murdered in 1893.

quoted George Knowles, Rochford Council Clerk, as saying that some of the 19th-century weather-boarded houses in North Street were a 'load of old rubbish and should be pulled down'. Two of these run-down properties were used for storage and one as a charity shop. The minister of the church opposite the buildings said at a public enquiry that Rochford was in danger of becoming a ghost town if the tumbledown properties were not demolished. Mr Ferguson, who ran the butcher's shop next door, had his appeal to demolish the buildings turned down, so after 33 years he closed his shop. The buildings were boarded up and the once-delightful, picturesque houses were covered with corrugated iron. Residents were

129 Buildings on the east side of the Square were demolished to make way for modern shops.

130 The ancient buildings have been pulled down, giving a view into North Street.

horrified to find, early one Sunday morning, workmen in the Square demolishing the old Hartley's Saddlers shop, built in 1777. Nothing could be done to stop them as it was impossible to obtain an injunction on a Sunday. On what the *Southend Standard* called 'Bloody Sunday', two of Rochford's oldest buildings were torn down without the permission or knowledge of the local authorities. This act of vandalism led to all relevant properties in the town being listed and made safe from the developers.

It was during the depressing 1970s, when properties were boarded up and some of the shops in the Square were demolished, that a group of shopkeepers decided it was time to re-open the market. It had re-opened during the First World War for the sale of farm stock, and closed again in 1959. There was a great deal of confusion and controversy about the latest suggestion. Some shopkeepers thought it would ruin their trade; others that it might bring more people into the town and increase their business. The motion to open the market was carried by one vote at a meeting of the Chamber of Trade. One member stormed out and many more were undecided. After three years the Chamber of Trade decided to abandon the project and Mr Reg Janes, manager of Reeve's Timber Merchants in North Street, formed a company to take on the market alone. He claimed it would bring many new people into the town. There were hundreds of applications for stalls and by 1977 Rochford market was back in business. TV 'personality' Monty Modlyn cut the ribbon and declared it officially open. The market, held every Tuesday, still proves very popular.

There had been little house building in the town because the sewers would be unable to cope. When a new sewage plant was built

131 House at the end of North Street. Market Alley is on the right.

off Stambridge Road, towards Ballards Gore, the rural council lifted the embargo and Rochford anticipated a building boom. New estates were put up on the outskirts of the town. The Holt Farm Estate, Holt Farm School and, later, St Theresa's School were built off Ashingdon Road, bringing more people and more traffic into the area. The new parish church of St Theresa was built in Ashingdon Road, replacing the church on the corner of Roche Avenue.

In the early '70s Whitehall spent over £1,000,000 deciding which was the best site for the third London Airport. The Town and Country Planning Association put in plans for a 3,000-acre site on the Maplin Sands on the coast to the east of Rochford, and submitted proposals to Rochford Council for a single runway airport on the reclaimed land. The plan would have required two new motorways to London. The 'anti-Maplin' protesters argued that a huge amount of valuable farmland would be lost. The Ministry of Defence establishment on Foulness Island would have to close and there was great concern over the thousands of birds, including the Brent geese, living in the Foulness area. Their habitat would be destroyed and great flocks of birds would be a danger to aircraft. Councillor Derek Woods was insistent that the airport would never be sited on Maplin as it was the most stupid plan he had ever seen. By October 1981 the idea had been abandoned but a year later the plan was re-opened. New rail and road links to London were discussed at the most expensive enquiry in history. The new airport, it was argued, would turn Southend into an important regional centre, bringing in more business and creating thousands of jobs in

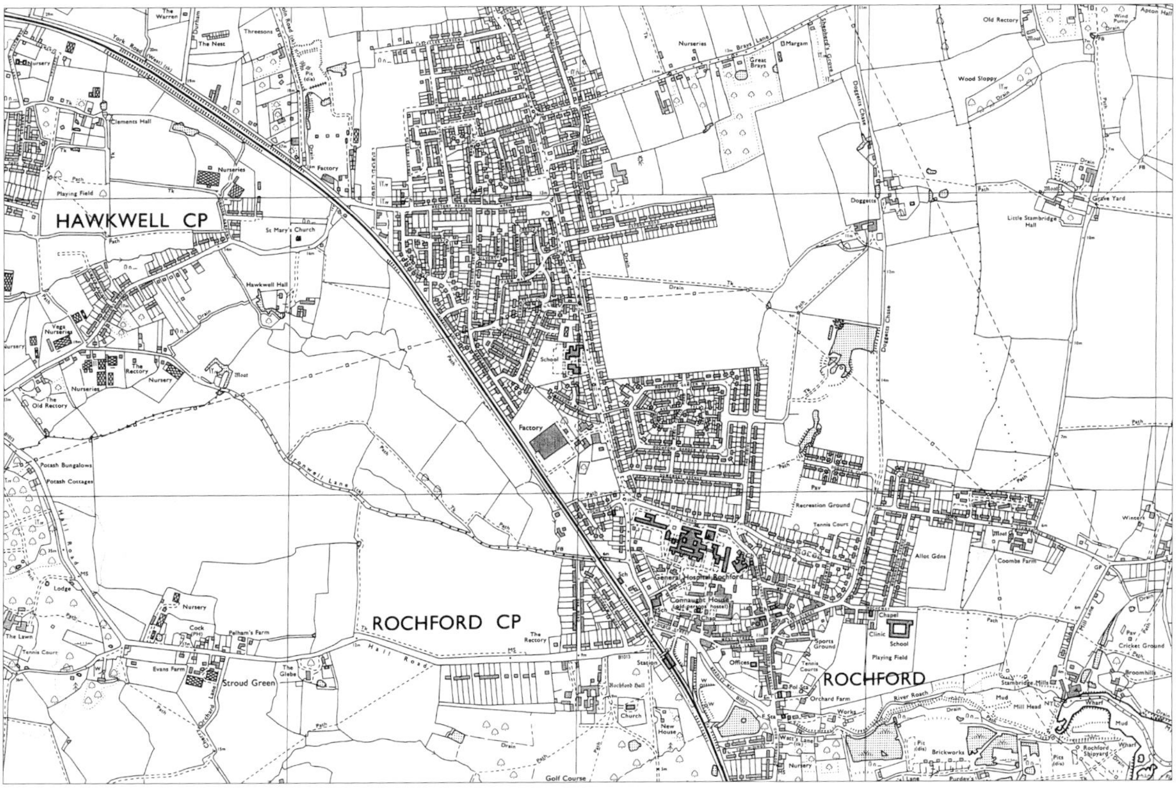

132 Map showing the extent of housing in 1971.

133 The Square. The building in the centre is the Market Bakery, established in 1825. The first shop on the left is the saddler's shop.

134 Aerial view of Rochford in the 1960s.

the surrounding area. The £3 billion scheme involved a deep water port with transport links to the A13. A huge car park would be built and a tunnel taking travellers from the airport to London would surface at Southend and Basildon. Once again Rochford began its fight against the airport. After 17 years of battle by one of the most powerful pressure groups ever known, Maplin was abandoned and the third airport was sited at Stansted.

An article in the local paper, the *Southend Standard*, in 1981 said that Rochford, Hockley, Barling and Hawkwell were on the brink of oblivion under proposed government reforms. The plan was to carve up local government boundaries, and divide Essex into 14 councils: Southend would be the biggest; Rayleigh, Rochford, Benfleet and Canvey would be combined. Eventually it was agreed that Canvey and Benfleet should become one council and Rayleigh and Rochford another. The District of Rochford was formed, which comprised the whole of the former Rayleigh Urban District and Rochford Rural District Councils. It was divided into 23 wards with 40 councillors. The Parliamentary representative was Bernard Braine. The changes, known as the 'Great Centralisation Plan', were unpopular in Rayleigh, as the majority of services were moved to Rochford. Plans had to be made to accommodate the displaced council staff. £55,000 was spent on buying Acacia House from the health authority and the former hospital staff house was turned into offices. The sale included access to three acres of land earmarked for housing. All the property in South Street from Acacia House to the Old House was now converted into offices for council staff.

The Old House, the most ancient property in Rochford, had been in a very bad state of repair for many years, the owner unable to afford its upkeep. The grade II listed ten-bedroomed

135 Southend Road, looking towards South Street, before the bypass.

home, valued at £18,000, was bought in 1982 by the council as a late medieval house, but as restoration progressed it became obvious that it was much older than at first thought. The house became a designated grade 1 listed building, and now forms part of the council offices.

The District Council of Rochford was granted armorial bearings in 1975. The shield is divided into 12 parts to symbolise the 12 original parishes. The Tudor rose is a reminder of Tudor influences, the sheaf of corn symbolises the importance of agriculture in the district, the crest depicts the mill at Rayleigh, and the notched sword is from the arms of Essex. On the left, the bull is a reference to the Bullen or Boleyn family. The wyvern on the right was part of the arms of Rayleigh Urban District Council. The motto 'Our Heritage, Our Future' was chosen from entries in a competition won by Mrs A. Littlewood from Prittlewell. The new Rochford Council wanted to form connections with the continent, preferably with a town of similar name, possibly Roquefort in France or Rochefort in Belgium; after a great deal of deliberation it was eventually decided to twin with Haltern in Germany.

After the reorganisation of local government, Rochford Town Hall, originally the Court House, became redundant. Being a listed building, its future uses were limited. It was necessary to sell the property in order to develop the old freight shed, built in the 1890s, an excellent example of Victorian railway architecture. The Freight House was

136 Armorial bearings were granted to the District of Rochford in 1975.

137 Rochford Rural District Council offices, formerly the Court House.

138 The Queen's Silver Jubilee Celebrations, 1977.

139 Felicity Jane finally closed in 2003.

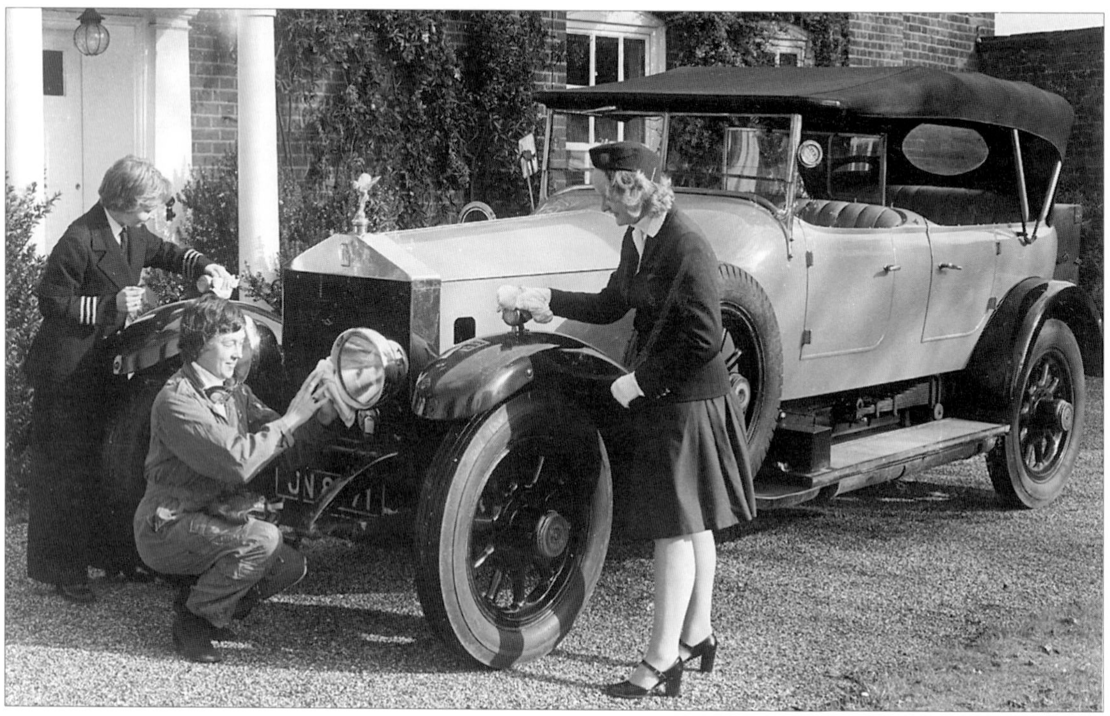

140 Anne Boulter, centre, chair of the British Women's Pilots Association, helps polish Mr Tabor's 1918 Rolls Royce outside Sutton Hall, ready for the Lord Mayor's Show of 1976.

completely renovated, keeping some of its original features, and officially opened again in 1982 as a venue for weddings, exhibitions, meetings and banquets.

The only offer received for the Court House was from a consortium of Freemasons. It was sold to them for £85,000 and they acquired the building on April Fool's Day, 1981. The lodge had moved to the Court House when it was purchased by Rochford Council in 1929 after the court transferred to Southend. The first lodge in the town, the Lodge of True Friendship, originally held its meetings at the *Old Ship* on the Tuesday on or before the full moon. One of the members, John Allen, the carpenter who made the last whispering post, lived at 24 South Street, a cottage which had been demolished to make room for the Court House.

In November 1978 Rochford was shocked by the news that there had been a brutal murder in the town. The victim, Mrs Trott, had been found in the bushes near Ship Lane, battered to death in a sex attack. Norah Trott, a well-known personality in Rochford, had been a founder member of the Chamber of Trade. She lived above her dress shop 'Felicity Jane' in North Street. The police were searching for a young, tall, slim man aged between 18 and 25 and described as having light brown hair and a pointed nose. He had been seen running down North Street and into East Street. Fifty police and a support team of 200 detectives set about finding Mrs Trott's killer. In the biggest murder hunt ever seen at that time, Essex police held 4,000 interviews at murder headquarters in the British Legion Hall in East Street. Detectives knocked on every door in Rochford. The killer was thought to be a local man as he knew his way through the alleyway. Sixty-three-year-old Norah was going to visit a friend in Westcliff when the attack took place. The police were convinced they knew the identity of the murderer but lacked the evidence to prove it. No one was ever convicted of the crime. Twenty-five years after the murder new evidence emerged after an anonymous letter was sent to the police. The case was re-opened and investigations are still ongoing. A man has been charged with the murder.

Thirteen

Into the New Millennium

Despite the new housing and re-opening of the market, Rochford in the early 1980s was still in a state of depression; several shops were empty, some boarded up, and the whole town looked neglected. Rochford Council's next plan to bring life back into the town involved a splendid new development with shops and a huge supermarket, the rear of which was to be on Back Lane, the front on what is now the car park. The little community of caravan dwellers who lived on the Locks Hill site had to be moved and the site was closed in 1974. This land provided parking space for 300 vehicles and a walkway to take shoppers through to the Square; two new office sites were to be built fronting the Bradley Way bypass. But the supermarket scheme met with the disapproval of many shopkeepers from Rochford and Hawkwell, who thought it would ruin their trade and force many small shops to close, and the project was eventually abandoned.

However, there were some improvements and signs of progress in the town. Approval was given in 1984 for a restaurant, conference centre and hotel, which was jointly owned by Derek Renouf and Thorpe Bay insurance

141 *Renouf's Hotel* and Conference Centre.

142 The award-winning new building at Horner's Corner.

underwriter John Edwards. Derek Renouf had formerly run a restaurant in South Street, next to Acacia House. On the ground floor were the conference centre, lounge, lobby, a bedroom for disabled visitors and a restaurant which catered for 120 diners. The 18 bedrooms were situated on the first floor. Work on Back Lane car park to prepare for the hotel cost £30,000. The neglected building on the junction of all four main roads had been a butcher's shop with an abattoir at the back for many years. The shop was named after the owner and has had several name changes. It was called Webster's Corner, then Palmer's Corner, and then Horner's Corner after brothers Jack and Harry Horner, who ran the shop for 20 years. They left when the building was compulsorily purchased by Rochford District Council for a new road scheme which never came to anything. Council plans to demolish it were

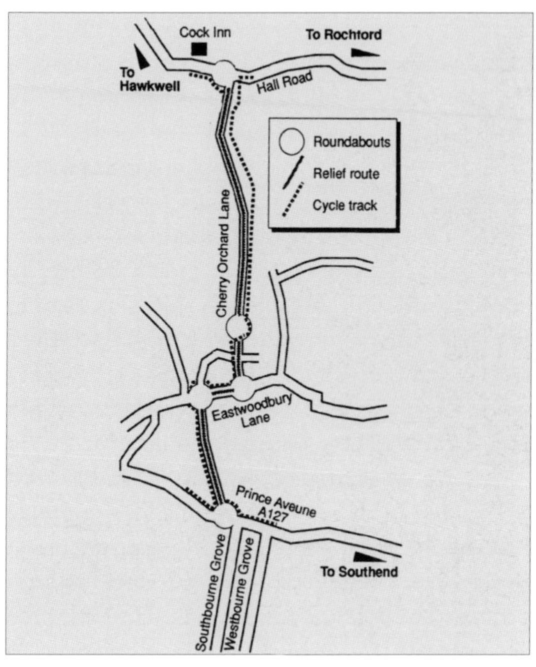

143 Plan of the Cherry Orchard relief road.

144 The part of the hospital once containing the maternity unit is now converted into St Luke's sheltered housing complex.

halted when it was discovered that, although the building was of no great historic value, the road junction was unique – one of the few cruciform road junctions in the country. The property remained boarded up for years until in 1985 it was bought by Lawrence Chapman, who wanted to restore it. He died before he could realise his dream, but his son Adrian fulfilled his father's ambition and tastefully redesigned and rebuilt the old shop. Adrian's grade II listed achievement won Rochford's award for the best restored building in 2001.

After a fierce battle by residents and against the wishes of most of the councillors, approval was finally given for a new housing estate on the former Matchbox site. Fairview Homes proposed to build houses, bedsits, flats and three access roads off Ashingdon Road, adding to the huge volume of traffic through Rochford's narrow streets. The Council came up with six schemes for a new road to divert some of the traffic from the town. Two of them would mean demolishing houses; the others involved cutting through the Roach Valley Conservation Areas and bringing the road close to 100 houses. Public meetings were arranged at the Freight House and Prince Avenue School, Westcliff, where plans were on show and the public was able to choose the preferred route. The Cherry Orchard Lane road was by far the most popular, but not with everyone. An *Evening Echo* reporter described it as 'the Highway to Hell'. It was proposed to develop the market garden at Eastwood and build a huge Tesco hyperstore with 700 parking spaces, a petrol station and a big hotel on the A127 opposite the end of Southbourne Grove, the £9 million road being built with proceeds of the sale of

145 This listed hospital chimney was saved from demolition.

the site. Southend Council rejected the plan, but after a ten-year delay the government gave the green light to the scheme and the bypass, from Hall Road through to Eastwood, across Eastwoodbury Lane and on to the A127, the first in the county to incorporate a cycle track, was finally under way. The 1½-mile road was officially opened in 1996.

In 1991 plans were revealed to centralise Rochford and Southend hospitals in the name of greater efficiency. The treasury gave permission to Southend Health Council Trust to borrow £27 million for extensive alterations at Southend. The scheme meant that half of Rochford Hospital would have to be closed and sold to make way for a multi-million pound development on the site. This included a huge supermarket and large housing development which would help fund the new extension that was to be added to Southend

146 The Town Clock being removed for repairs.

General Hospital. The public were outraged. Hundreds of Rochford residents worked at the hospital and many more relied on it for a living; shopkeepers, pub and restaurant owners depended on hospital staff and visitors to the hospital for part of their livelihood. The 'Save our Hospital Campaign' began. Protesters claimed their first victory when English Heritage submitted a recommendation that part of the hospital was architecturally important and should be grade II listed: the Boiler House with its huge chimney, the main hospital block and Johnson Ward were safe from demolition. Southend National Health Service Trust's plans were disrupted by this and no supermarket chain showed any interest in building on the site. The Trust put up 'for sale' notices in a desperate attempt to recover some of the money they needed and faced an 18-month deadline to sell the site.

The battle to save the hospital carried on for the next four years with notices, meetings and media coverage. At one time the nurses formed a human chain around the site. But in 1995 the future of the hospital was decided: the maternity wards would be turned into a nursing home with sixty *en suite* rooms, Johnson Ward would be converted into houses and flats and Chalkwell Ward would be demolished. Sixty-six houses, six bungalows and a two-storey block of special needs homes would be built. The listed chimney and boiler house would become elegant luxury apartments. The largest cottage hospital in the country was to go and nurses and other staff were transferred to Southend. The move was a major blow to the economy of Rochford. On Friday 13 November the last vestiges of the hospital were transferred to Southend and by 24 November the bulldozers were at work. It is ironic that, in 2002, a headline in the local newspaper said that selling Rochford Hospital may have been a great mistake.

The double-faced clock on the W.I. Hall had to be removed for repair and was missing for its centenary. The clock has been a local landmark since 1897, when it was bought to celebrate the Diamond Jubilee of Queen Victoria, and locals were delighted when it was returned.

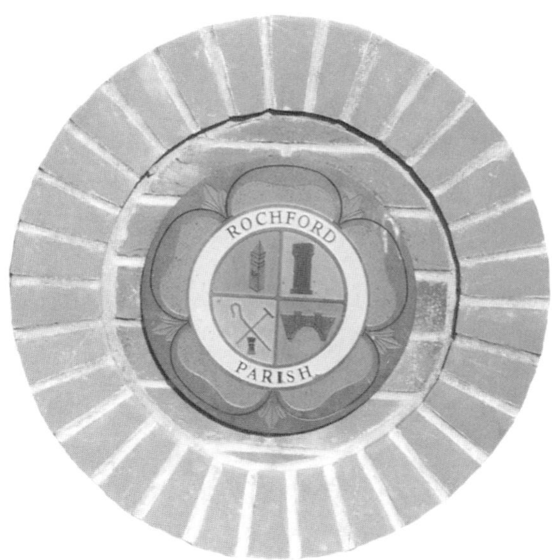

147 The parish sign designed by the Butterley Brick Company was unveiled in 1991 on the junction of Bradley Way and South Street. The bricks were made at the brickworks in Cherry Orchard Lane. The bronze plaque depicts the Whispering Post, a chimney from the Hall, farm implements and Salt Bridge.

To celebrate the 750th anniversary of the granting of the royal market charter, the Rochford Hundred Festival Committee organised a grand Medieval Fair in the reservoir park and the Old House gardens, with stalls, potters, dancers, fortune tellers and a hog roast. A huge black glove hanging in the tree denoted that 'at Michaelmas in September a great glove stands to represent the handshake of promises, the welcome to buyers and sellers'.

The new century began with fireworks, a fête and the refurbishment of the Square. There had been many proposals to pedestrianise the latter but all had faced opposition from shoppers and shopkeepers, as it would mean no parking spaces. Now the pavements were widened, ramps for the disabled were built, and seats, railings and new street lights were put in

148 The replica pump is put in place in the Square. The pump was made and donated by Adrian Chapman.

149 The horse trough was returned from Hockley Woods to the Square in 2002.

place. The horse trough which was presented to the parish in 1904 to commemorate the coronation of Edward VII had been in the Square and in constant use until the late 1950s, but, when there was no longer a need for it, it had been banished to Hockley Woods. It was now brought back and filled with flowers. A replica of the old Town Pump was made and donated by Adrian Chapman. The tumbledown forge in Back Lane, used by the *King's Head* in its coaching inn days, was pulled down to make way for a private house. Work began on three shops in West Street, which had been taken over by Southend District Trust after a long and complicated legal battle ended in a compulsory purchase order. They would become five cottages.

150 Work on the ancient cottages in West Street.

151 Rumbelows, the electrical shop, has been boarded and empty for years and still awaits its ultimate fate.

The problem of the Rumbelows building dragged on, however. Rumbelows, one of the biggest shops in West Street, plus a cottage, nos. 50 to 54 West Street, had been empty since the electrical company left in 1993. The building, much damaged by fire, had been partly boarded up and partly left to the elements and it was the source of many arguments over its future. An Orsett-based development company wanted to replace the building and cottage with modern replicas; the Southend and District Preservation Trust wanted to save as much of the old building as possible and restore the property. A fierce battle between the two groups raged for years, finally coming to an end on 17 December 2002, when the council voted that the building should be restored.

The airport caused a furore again when bosses wanted to turn it into a major holiday flight centre. Hampered by the railway at one end of the runway and the 800-year-old St Lawrence Church at the other, they devised several plans, including taking the runway over the railway, a £50 million project which would close the railway for up to two years. Alternatively they could move the runway, demolishing the Golf Club and diverting the river, or demolishing the new Tesco supermarket, hotel and newly built bank. The favoured option was to move the ancient church and graveyard 100 metres from its present site and remove the spire, but the proposal brought hundreds of complaints from the public, and a letter from Prince Charles to

152 The market is still thriving.

the vicar expressing his dismay and wishing the campaigners every success. The perimeter of the church was festooned with yellow ribbons and an English Heritage spokesman was doubtful that the building could be moved. Enormous technical challenges would have to be faced before any decision could be made. The cottages which had prevented the expansion in the 1960s would be pulled down, but the fate of the church and the airport remain undecided.

The fate of the hospital, however, is finally resolved. Part of the old Rochford Hospital,

153 Plans to move St Lawrence Church have caused great controversy.

154 The BP garage and shop closed in 2002.

155 The future of the police station in South Street is uncertain.

156 Occupied for many years by Angus Grant, then Chemys, this shop in South Street has been empty for some time.

closed for 11 years, is to be reopened and work has begun on demolishing some of the abandoned buildings. It was proposed that £22 million should be spent on building new mental health wards. Runwell Hospital will close and the patients will be transferred to Rochford. Four of the old buildings will be refurbished and brought up to 21st-century standards and 148 more beds will be made available. The project should bring new life to Rochford. Over 400 new jobs will be created. Plans for building an old people's complex, over a hundred flats and a supermarket have been revealed on part of the site, which have met again with disapproval from many of the public.

157 The sign over the door of the abandoned Lisa Marie reads 'International Jewellers'.

158 The Mill.

159 St Andrew's Church.

One development plan to receive no objections is the Cherry Orchard Jubilee Country Park, the first in the district, which has received grants from the Forestry Commission and Thames Gateway South Essex (which offers a great opportunity to regenerate and revitalise South Essex). Thousands of trees have been planted so far and there will be an orchard and a lake. The country park, offering unparalleled views across the surrounding countryside, was officially opened by Princess Anne in March 2003. Perhaps in the 21st century Rochford will find its former importance, and win back its unique market town character. To quote Cryer, 'The past has gone; that which has fallen will never be replaced.' It is up to us to preserve that which is left.

Bibliography

Benton, Philip, *The History of the Rochford Hundred 1867-88* (reprinted 1991)
Brake, George T., *The Scene of Early Methodism in the Rochford Hundred* (1994)
Church guides from Ashingdon, Canewdon, Paglesham, Rochford and Stambridge
Clark, Dr Michael, *Rochford Hall* (1990)
Cryer, L.R., *A History of Rochford* (1978)
English, Jacqueline A. (compiler), *The Old House* (1984)
Essex County Council, *Origins of Rochford* (2000)
Harriott, John, *Struggles through Life* (1815)
Hunt, Leslie, *The History of Southend Airport* (1993)
Janes, R. and D. and L. Reeve, *Rochford Market* (1979)
Jerram-Burrows, L.E., *Bygone Rochford* (1988)
Jerram-Burrows, L., *Rochford Remembers* (1983)
Morant, Philip, *The History and Antiquities of the County of Essex* (1876, reprinted 1978)
Reynolds, Dr David, *Old Rochford Hospital* (1995)
Sipple, Mavis, *Titbits and Tales of Old Essex* (1999)
Sipple, Mavis, *Extraordinary Essex* (2000)
Sipple, Mavis, *Titbits and Tales of Essex Inns* (2001)
Williamson, David, *Kings and Queens of Britain* (1991)
Wittingham, Peter, *Rochford Past and Present* (audio tape, 1989-90)
Yearsley, Ian, *A History of Southend* (2001)

Index

Page numbers printed in **bold** type refer to illustrations.